A Guide to Effective Communication

Edited by
Pamela D. Hopkins
East Carolina University

KENDALL/HUNT PUBLISHING COMPANY
4050 Westmark Drive P.O. Box 1840 Dubuque, Iowa 52004-1840

Copyright © 2005 by Pamela D. Hopkins

ISBN 0-7575-2094-4

Kendall/Hunt Publishing Company has the exclusive rights to reproduce this work,
to prepare derivative works from this work, to publicly distribute this work,
to publicly perform this work and to publicly display this work.

All rights reserved. No part of this publication may be reproduced,
stored in a retrieval system, or transmitted, in any form or by any
means, electronic, mechanical, photocopying, recording or otherwise,
without the prior written permission of Kendall/Hunt Publishing Company.

Printed in the United States of America
10 9 8 7 6 5 4 3 2 1

Contents

School of Communication Syllabus   v
Common Course Syllabus   vi

Course Assignments   xi
Informative Presentation (15%)   xi
Group Presentation (20%)   xii
Persuasive Presentation (20%)   xiii
Interview Exercise (15%)   xiv

Communication Tools Essential to Winning a Job Offer   1
Understanding the Job Search Process   1
Is Your Resume a Piece of Marketing?   4
Creating Letters That Market You Effectively   13
Job Interviewing—The True Test of Your Communication Skills   25
Communicating Effectively Using Stories—SACs   36
Generating Questions to Ask   39
Have a Positive Attitude   44
Review of Communication Tools Essential to Winning the Job   45

Group Work   47
One Group Work Assignment (4 Groups)   47
Peer Group Evaluation   49
Peer Evaluation Form   50

Managing Anxiety   51
Changing Cognition   52
The Cycle of Speech Anxiety   53
Examples of Stinking Thinking   54
Physical Tools for Managing Speech Anxiety   56
Tips for Managing Anxiety   58
Visualization Exercise   59

Choosing a Speech Topic   61
Washed Out and Overdone Topics   61
The Topic   63

Audience Analysis   65
What Is Audience Analysis and Why Is It Important?   65

Speaker Credibility 67
Tips for Speaker Credibility 67
Elements in the Aristotelian Model 67

Informative Speaking 68
Guidelines for Informative Speeches 68
Pointers for Your Informative Speech 69
Public Speaking Do's and Don'ts for Executives 70
Example of an Informative Speech Assignment 73

Persuasive Speaking 75
Guidelines for Persuasive Speeches 75
Pointers for Your Persuasive Speech 75
Example of a Persuasive Speech Assignment 77

Speech Outlines 79
Persuasive Sales Speech 79
Sample Outline for a Persuasive Speech Using Monroe's Motivated Sequence Method 81
Sample Outline Format: Monroe's Motivated Sequence 85
Informative Speech Outline 87
Persuasive Speech Outline 89
Specific Purpose and Central Idea Exercises 91

Speech Preparation 92
How Do I Get There from Here? 92
Toastmasters International "Be Prepared to Speak" Checklist 94
Tips for Speaking 98
Tips for Speaking . . . The Second Time! 99

Evaluation Forms 101
Peer Review: Informative Speaking 103
Peer Review: Persuasive/Persuasive Sales 111
Monroe's Motivated Sequence Evaluation Form 119

Speech Delivery 121
Articulation Exercise 121
Tongue Twisters 121
More Tongue Twisters 122
Common Pronunciation Mistakes 123

Self-Critique 124
Sample Self-Critique #1 124
Sample Self-Critique #2 125
Example of a Self-Critique Assignment 127

School of Communication Syllabus

Because COMM 2420 is taught in multiple sections, it is essential that requirements are consistent across the board. Therefore, this is the common syllabus for all COMM 2420 classes. Your instructor will also give you an individual syllabus with a course schedule. They might add to the policies and procedures stated in the common syllabus or they might add an un-graded assignment. You need to read both the common syllabus and the instructor's individual syllabus carefully and more than once. Make yourself familiar with the rules of the course—it will save time and eliminate confusion on your part later in the semester.

EAST CAROLINA UNIVERSITY

College of Fine Arts and Communication

School of Communication

Greenville, NC 27858

COMMON COURSE SYLLABUS
COMM 2420: Business and Professional Communication (3 s.h.) (GE:FA)

Course Description

COMM 2420 Emphasis on developing excellent communication skills in everyday speaking, interviews, group presentations and public speaking. Student organizes and delivers informative, persuasive, and group presentations.

Competencies/Objectives

This course reflects the following School of Communication competencies that will prepare students for professional experiences in diverse organizational settings:

- Understand multiple theoretical perspectives and diverse intellectual underpinnings in communication as reflected in its philosophy and/or history;
- Communicate effectively with diverse others;
- Create and deliver presentations in several forms such as oral, written, broadcast, online, and/or multimedia;
- Reflectively construct and analyze arguments and discourse intended to influence beliefs, attitudes, values, and practices;
- Conduct systematic inquiry;
- Analyze and practice ethical communication;
- Apply effective approaches to human relational interaction in various settings.

In order to achieve the aforementioned competencies, students will carry out the following objectives:

- Recognize the role of self in communication;
- Analyze and discuss self-presentations and those of others for communication effectiveness by providing reflection and feedback;
- Construct and deliver presentations common to the expectations of diverse organizational settings that adhere to the fundamental practices of public speaking;

- Demonstrate critical thinking;
- Demonstrate cultural sensitivity and use language that responds to diversity;
- Develop communication competence that effectively responds to the contextual rules and norms of a variety of communication settings;
- Develop active listening skills;
- Distinguish among various forms of research, evaluate and synthesize them into supporting evidence appropriate to the communicative situation;
- Employ the theoretical perspectives relevant to group processes and interpersonal interactions;
- Recognize the various components of the communication process in organizational settings;
- Employ techniques to manage communication anxiety in various contexts;
- Prepare presentations that reflect ethics in communication.

Course Requirements and Weights

Informative Presentation	15%
Group Presentation	20%
Persuasive Presentation	20%
Interview Exercise	15%
Exams	20%
Attendance/Participation	10%
Total	100%

Grading Criteria

Reflective of the various items stated on the individual evaluation forms for the informative, group and persuasive presentations, the instructor will take the synthesis of the following elements into consideration:

1. A topic that is appropriate to the speech purpose, time constraints, audience and occasion;
2. A clear organizational pattern;
3. An extemporaneous delivery that is fluid and engaging;
4. A well-developed sentence outline;
5. Relevant supporting sources; and
6. Appropriate and professional attire.

University Grading Scale

A	90-100%
B	80-89%
C	70-79%
D	60-69%
F	below 60%

Methods of Teaching

This course is taught in a variety of formats to include lectures, collaborative activities, analysis of student performances, assisted media, and discussion.

Materials

O'Hair, D., Friedrich, G., & Dixon, L. (2004). *Strategic Communication in Business and the Professions* (5th ed.). Boston: Houghton Mifflin.

Classroom Policies

Attendance

Students are expected to attend punctually all class sessions. Absences are counted from the first class meeting, and absences because of late registration will not be automatically excused. The student is held accountable for the work covered in each class meeting whether absences are excused or not.

Each instructor shall determine the class attendance policy for each of his or her courses. This policy, along with other course requirements, will be presented to the class, preferably in writing, at the beginning of the semester or summer school term.

The Student Health Service does not issue official written excuses for illness or injury except in the case of final examination when a grade of incomplete (I) is recommended. Upon request, however, the Student Health Service will confirm that the student has received medical care. If a faculty member needs additional information regarding the nature and/or scope of an illness or injury, the student must authorize the release of the information by signing a release of information form in the Student Health Service.

Instructors are expected to recognize and honor university-excused absences, i.e., treat the absence as an excused absence. Instructors may require that students provide reasonable advanced notice of a university-excused absence, when possible. If required by the instructor, verification of a university-excused absence may be obtained by students contacting the university's ombudsman.

The death of an immediate family member or student participation in religious holidays may be considered an excused absence under university policy. Should such a circumstance occur, and the faculty member desires verification, the student should contact the university's ombudsman for a university-excused absence and provide documentation of the particulars.

The university's ombudsman *may* authorize university-excused absences for activities as follows:

1. Participation in authorized university activities as an official representative of the university (i.e., sporting events, delegate to regional or national meetings or conferences, participation in necessary travel to and from university-sponsored performances);
2. Participation in activities directly related to university course work as part of the course requirements; or
3. Participation in other activities deemed by the university's ombudsman to meet the spirit of these requirements by furthering the mission and enhancing the reputation of East Carolina University.

Except as provided above, requests for a university-excused absence should be submitted, whenever possible to the university's ombudsman at least a week prior to the scheduled absence. Requests submitted after the fact will be disapproved unless circumstances made prior approval impossible or unreasonable.

Mandatory Days

1. Students must attend class on ALL scheduled presentation days, including other students' presentations and group project days, and exam days.
2. Points deducted on mandatory days will be determined by the instructor.
3. Any additional mandatory days are a choice of the individual instructor.
4. Exam dates cannot be changed.

Make-up Assignments

All work must be completed as scheduled. A student who fails to give his/her presentation or misses an exam on the day scheduled because of a legitimate emergency *MAY POSSIBLY BUT NOT NECESSARILY* be excused after the fact. The instructor reserves the right to determine what is deemed legitimate.

If the absence qualifies as a university excused absence, proper documentation MUST be provided reasonably in advance. The instructor MAY then allow the student to make up the presentation or exam.

Academic Integrity

Academic integrity is expected of every East Carolina University student. Academically violating the Honor Code consists of the following: cheating, plagiarism, falsification and attempts. Procedures governing academic integrity violations are described in *The Student Handbook Online* and in the *Faculty Manual*.

Student Conduct

Students enrolled at East Carolina University are expected to uphold at all times standards of academic integrity and personal behavior that will reflect credit upon themselves, their families, and East Carolina University. Students are also expected to behave with propriety and to respect the rights and privileges of others. They are expected to abide by the laws of the city, state, and nation and by all rules and regulations of ECU. Failure to do so may result in their being sanctioned by or separated from the university.

Registration at the university implies the student's acceptance of the published academic regulations and all other rules found in any official publication or announcements. Conduct regulations, including the academic integrity policy, are described in *The Student Handbook Online*.

Language Discrimination

The School of Communication at East Carolina University requires the use of nonsexist and nondiscriminatory language in written and oral communication by students and faculty. Profane and offensive language will not be tolerated.

Classroom Behavior

It is a violation of University policy (and North Carolina law) to bring weapons, drugs, or animals into a University building. These items are strictly prohibited, especially as visual aids.

Submission of Assignments

All assignments must be typed or computer generated unless otherwise noted by your instructor.

Disability Services

East Carolina University seeks to comply fully with the Americans with Disabilities Act (ADA). Students requesting accommodations based on a covered disability must go to the Department for Disability Support Services, located in Brewster A-117, to verify the disability before any accommodations can occur. The telephone number is 252-328-6799.

Emergency Weather

In the event of weather emergencies, students can access information about ECU through the following sources: ECU emergency notices *http://www.ecu.edu/alert* or the ECU emergency information hotline: 252-328-0062.

Course Assignments

INFORMATIVE PRESENTATION (15%)

Dress:
Professional attire

Time:
Three to six minutes

Delivery:
Extemporaneous

Organization:
The presentation follows a clear chronological, spatial, topical, comparison-contrast, problem-solution, or cause-effect pattern along with an introduction, body, conclusion, clear thesis, support and transitions.

Planning:
The presentation will reflect research in the form of sources that are incorporated and cited fully in the presentation.

Outline:
Submit a well-developed outline to include (1) preliminary information (topic, general purpose, specific purpose, thesis, arrangement, main points), and (2) a *sentence outlined* introduction, body, and conclusion along with *internal and end references* properly cited. Choose APA or MLA as the style for citing sources. The rule in preparing a speaking outline (which you can later transcribe to note cards) is one sentence per denotation I. A.,1., a. i., etc.).

Visual Aid:
Presentations will include a useful, appropriate and professional visual aid (self, poster, overhead, object, picture, etc.) with which you should consider its *size* and demonstrate its *proper incorporation.*

Grading Criteria:
The instructor will take the synthesis of the following elements into consideration: a topic that is appropriate to the purpose of the presentation, time constraints, audience and occasion; organization of the presentation's introduction, body and conclusion; inclusion of strong transitions; extemporaneous delivery; quality and handling

of visual aid; appropriate support; citing of sources; use of note cards; verbal and nonverbal delivery; adherence to ethics; appropriate and culturally sensitive language; professional attire; and a sentence outline.

GROUP PRESENTATION (20%)

Dress:
Professional attire

Time:
Left to the instructor

Delivery:
Extemporaneous

Organization:
The presentation follows a clear chronological, spatial, topical, comparison-contrast, problem-solution, or cause-effect pattern along with an introduction, body, conclusion, clear thesis, support and transitions.

Planning:
Assembling yourselves in groups, you are to devise a thorough, organized, prepared and practiced presentation dealing with your assigned or chosen topic. You are encouraged to appeal to the various learning-styles of the audience by using a variety of approaches in disseminating the information to your peers. Please include an introduction, body and a conclusion. *Work as a whole unit* in structuring the presentation and scrutinizing what should or should not be included in the presentation. It is essential that you *engage* your audience.

Visual Aid:
Presentations will include a useful, appropriate and professional visual aid (self, poster, overhead, object, picture, etc.) with which you should consider its *size* and demonstrate its *proper incorporation.*

Grading Criteria:
The instructor will take the synthesis of the following elements into consideration: evidence of group collaboration; a topic that is appropriate to the purpose of the presentation, time constraints, audience and occasion; organization of the presentation's introduction, body and conclusion; inclusion of strong transitions; extemporaneous delivery; quality and handling of visual aid; appropriate support; citing of sources; use of note cards; verbal and nonverbal delivery; adherence to ethics; appropriate and culturally sensitive language; professional attire.

PERSUASIVE PRESENTATION (20%)

Dress:
Professional attire

Time:
Five to seven minutes

Delivery:
Extemporaneous

Organization:
The presentation follows a clear organizational pattern reflective of a persuasive presentation.

Planning:
The presentation will reflect research in the form of sources that are incorporated and cited fully in the presentation.

Outline:
Submit a well-developed outline to include (1) preliminary information (topic, general purpose, specific purpose, thesis, arrangement, main points), and (2) a *sentence outlined* introduction, body, and conclusion along with *internal and end references* properly cited. Choose APA or MLA as the style for citing sources. The rule in preparing a speaking outline (which you can later transcribe to note cards) is one sentence per denotation (I., A.,1., a. i., etc.).

Visual Aid:
Presentations will include a useful, appropriate and professional visual aid (self, poster, overhead, object, picture, etc.) with which you should consider its size and demonstrate its *proper incorporation.*

Grading Criteria:
The instructor will take the synthesis of the following elements into consideration: a topic that is appropriate to the purpose of the presentation, time constraints, audience and occasion; organization of the presentation's introduction, body and conclusion; inclusion of strong transitions; extemporaneous delivery; quality and handling of visual aid; appropriate support; citing of sources; use of note cards; verbal and nonverbal delivery; adherence to ethics; valid argument supported with evidence; presence of counterargument; appropriate and culturally sensitive language; professional attire; and a sentence outline.

INTERVIEW EXERCISE (15%)

Goal:

Whether for the purpose of information gathering or employment, at the bare minimum, the design of the COMM 2420 interview exercise(s) should seek to accomplish the following outcomes:

- Understand the roles of the interviewer and interviewee,
- Appreciate the significance of preparation,
- Understand the interview structure and procedures,
- Develop awareness of verbal and nonverbal portrayals and perceptions,
- Increase communication competence,
- Engage in active listening,
- Develop and ask effective and appropriate questions.

Note:

Instructor will provide specific details of assignment.

COMMUNICATION TOOLS ESSENTIAL TO WINNING A JOB OFFER

In today's society the job search process is much like selling a product. The job seeker is the product that must be sold, resumes and cover letters are product marketing, and the employer is the buyer. In order to win the job offer, you have to demonstrate that you can do the job, that you will ft in with the work team and you must differentiate in the mind of the prospective employer the differences between you and other job seekers. To accomplish this you must be able to communicate effectively!

UNDERSTANDING THE JOB SEARCH PROCESS

One of the most significant changes in today's job search process which affects people in career transition, is the necessity of knowing where you want to go and what you want to do. It used to be that because you knew you were looking for a job, you would focus on finding job openings. In today's job market you must identify your functional strengths (what you have to offer) and your industry preferences at the very onset of your job search. No longer can you prepare resumes and cover letters that simply present who you are and what you have done. Now they must be marketing materials that clearly communicate to prospective decision-makers what you can do to make a difference for their company.

The following is an outline of steps you could take as you begin your job search.

I. Develop a List of Companies in Your Targeted Field

A. Decide which broad industries to target based on your interests, experience, and work values.
B. Decide what geographical area(s) you want to consider.
C. Go to online resources like Hoover's (*www.hoovers.com*), Vault (*www.vault.com*) and WetFeet (*www.wetfeet.com*) and research the companies based on your preferences.

II. Rank Your Choices

A. Obtain enough information (number of employees, sales, primary products or services offered, and key decision-makers) to rank the companies. You need only enough information to determine whether each company can be ranked as an A, B, or C. There is no sense in doing in-depth research on a company, only to find out that they see no point in talking with you. Learn enough about the company to determine IF they are a good target. Save the in-depth research for when you get an *interview*. Is the company as big as you'd like? Are its sales revenues and net income increasing? Does it have a unique product? Are there branch offices in your chosen area?

Bruce E. Maxwell, M.Ed., N.C.C.

Copyright © Bruce Maxwell, 2004. Used with permission by the author.

B. Many job hunters start by looking in the phone book for local companies in their targeted field. Call for an information packet and get a Reference Librarian to help you find information on the company. The library will have access to any published articles and annual reports.
C. Compile your list of targeted companies:

A's—companies that interest you the most;
B's—companies you might want to pursue later;
C's—companies to drop or eliminate.

D. Work on your A's in alphabetical groups of between four and ten at a time unless they rank themselves for you in another way, such as location or fit with your experience. Go to the library and find any articles written in the last three years, copy them, and bring them home to read. Create a file for each company.

III. Start Using the Telephone

A. Obtain the name of the decision-maker over your area of expertise and their correct mailing address.
B. Talk to the customer service or public relations department about the company's products or services.
C. Talk to a customer who currently is using their products or services.
D. Talk to a sales representative.
E. Talk to a dealer or distributor and ask if you can evaluate the product personally.

IV. Contact the Decision-Maker at Targeted Companies

A. Put together a customized cover letter that highlights your functional strengths, briefly describes one or two of your accomplishments, and presents the ways in which you could benefit the company. Mail it along with a copy of your resume to the decision-maker.
B. Here's where the key verbal communication tools come in. About four days after you mail the letter (seven if sending it out of state), call the decision-maker. Follow these steps (and tools provided in this chapter) when making each call:
   1. Share your background and find a common ground to establish a relationship (a power greeting).
   2. Ask a series of probing questions that will identify the needs, problems, and challenges of the company/department (asking probing questions).
   3. Provide stories that relate how your past accomplishments are relevant to the company's needs (SACS).
   4. After at least five minutes (but no more than 20 minutes), suggest that you would like to get together face-to-face to talk about these issues in more depth and offer two specific days in the near future when you could meet with them. ("I would really like to get together with you face-to-face to talk about this in more depth. I'll be in your area over Spring Break. Would Tuesday, March 16th

or Thursday, March 18th be better for you?") Set a specific time for a MEETING (not an interview).

C. If after five unsuccessful attempts to reach the decision-maker, spaced over the course of the day, leave a message. If after leaving messages for three days in a row, the decision-maker still won't call you back, ask the assistant or secretary for help. Try to schedule a time in the decision-maker's calendar for another telephone conversation. Rejection is hard to take, but hang in there. In most cases, hiring managers are not disinterested, they are just busy.

D. Proceed with a phone conversation. Ask for a next step. Uncover any concerns the hiring manager might have. If there isn't a possibility of a position now, ask whether he/she thinks there might be one in the next year.

E. If you are unable to meet with the decision-maker, ask for referrals to other people with whom you can speak—people in other departments within the company, in a competitor's company, or perhaps customers who may be interested in someone with your talents.

V. Keep Yourself in the Running after a Meeting

A. After your meeting with the decision-maker, put together a three paragraph "After Interview Thank You" letter in which you thank him/her for taking the time to meet with you to emphasize:

1. What you can do to make a difference, in light of the problems you identified;
2. Those aspects of your background that seemed of particular interest;
3. Your sincere interest in being a part of this "team".

B. Tell the decision-maker that if you haven't heard from him/her in about ten days, you will call back to see "how the hiring process is going."

C. If after about ten days you haven't heard back, call to reaffirm your interest. It is important to keep your name in the forefront, and look for an opportunity to get together for another meeting. Express your interest in discussing in more depth ways you could help solve their problems or bring about needed change.

D. Keep checking back until you receive a definite yes or no. Ask how often you should check (they might be interviewing other candidates). If you are not being scheduled for a second interview, your chances at this point are small, so get your campaign back in high gear and continue your job search.

E. Sometimes the company is just not able to create a new position and must wait until the new budget. In that situation, the time it will take to generate an interview will be longer. If you get the impression that they are interested and do want to hire you but cannot do so at this time, look for ways to stay in contact. For example, you might fax a copy of a recent article you found in the library (a "just-thinking-of-you" fax).

F. Stay in touch. Call and check about once a quarter. If you haven't had any success after a year, drop them from your list.

IS YOUR RESUME A PIECE OF MARKETING?

As I have said before, getting a job is sales. You are both the product and the salesperson, and the resume is your advertising. The end result may be a job, but no one gets hired from a resume. As advertising, the purpose of the resume is to cause the employer to want to talk with you enough to invite you for an interview. There is no "right way" to put together a resume; many different styles can be effective. A sure way to know if your resume is working is whether or not it is getting you interviews.

Jobs exist because employers have a need, a problem, or challenge that they want to resolve by hiring an employee. In other words, they need someone to do something for them. Your resume should let the employer know that you can help solve his/her problems. Simply listing your education and work experience will probably not convey this information. You must also tell the employer what you could do in your area of expertise to help them solve their problems. As advertising, your resume does just that: it **advertises** how you can help employers solve their problems and why they might want to pay you a living wage to get that problem solved.

> **RULE OF THUMB**
> You know how effective your resume is by the number of interviews you are getting

A good resume accomplishes three goals. It tells the employer: (1) what you can do in their field, (2) what you have done that relates to the job, and (3) your qualifications for the job.

A resume is like a map. You have to lead the reader through each aspect of your resume. It should describe your objective, capabilities, education, experience, and qualifications. Ideally in each part of your resume, you will present information that will make the reader want to read more!

Students are often afraid they can not land a good job because they do not have significant work experience. Realize that what you are selling is **potential** You have as much potential as the next person. Your resume is a tool to communicate that potential.

> **RULE OF THUMB**
> If the information is important to the employer it belongs on your resume; if it's not, throw it out!

Go to *http://online.onetcenter.org* which is a database of job descriptions in order to learn what an employer would hire you to do. Review the tasks typical of those positions.

Decide which tasks are your strongest. Condense the phrases down into resume suitable tasks and list them in a Professional Summary or Capabilities Profile section.

If you are pursuing jobs in several different fields, you may end up with several different resumes. Prepare one resume for each type of job you are pursing, each emphasizing the different capabilities required by that field. As you describe the work you have done in the different positions you have held, use action verbs to communicate effectiveness.

Styles

Resumes typically fit one of four styles: chronological, functional, accomplishment, or Curriculum Vita (CV). You may also run into employers who request a scanable resume. A scanable resume is not an additional style; rather, it is a specific format that allows any resume to be read by a scanning device.

The chronological style presents information in chronological (oldest listed first to most recent) or reverse chronological order (most recent listed first and then going backwards in time) your job-related volunteer and work experiences.

Functional resumes group your skills and experiences together based on job-related functional areas regardless of when they occurred.

Accomplishment-based resumes list your experiences in reverse chronological order and include examples of the achievements and successes you have had with each employer.

> **RULE OF THUMB**
> Place the information on the resume in order of its importance to the employer.

The Curriculum Vita is used exclusively for teaching in higher education. Go to the Career Management office on campus for help if you decide you need to write a CV.

The challenge is knowing which type of resume is best for you to use in a particular job-search situation. You can use the Resume Decision Tree as a guide for making that decision. In some situations you might even need to use a style different from the one recommended. You will need to determine which style is best based on your research into the position, the employer, and the location.

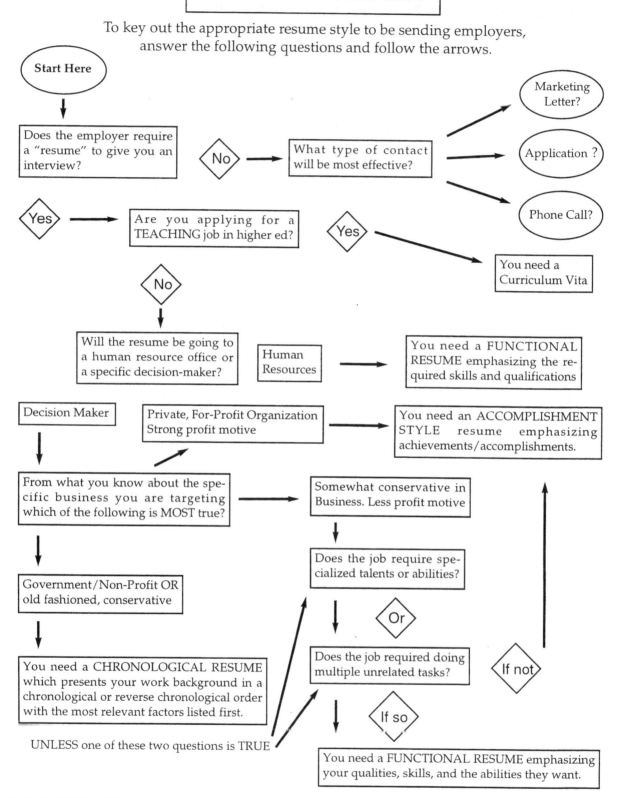

Copyright © Bruce Maxwell, 2004.

Reverse Chronological Resume

SIMON E. ANDREWS

2301 Hidden Meadow Dr., Fuquay-Varina, NC 27526
Home (919) 447-0546   Mobile (919) 538-9957
seandrews@aol.com

Objective:
A full-time position as a Project Superintendent for a commercial construction firm where I can use my skills in planning, estimating, and materials management.

Professional Summary
A experienced professional, with two years of construction management experience and a demonstrated ability to select, train and retain self-motivated employees. I offer you a solid understanding of managing employees in a multi-tasking environment, strong written and oral communication skills, experience in developing and implementing quality control programs, the ability to prepare and submit budget estimates and progress and cost tracking reports, and a strong interest in planning, organizing, and directing construction activities.

Education
Bachelor of Science, Construction Management, East Carolina University,   May 2006

Minor—Business Administration

GPA 3.4

Selected Coursework: Construction Techniques, Construction Materials, AutoCAD Design, Physics, Trigonometry, Estimating, Surveying, Contracts and Specifications, Architectural Plans and Analysis, Structural Analysis.

Work Experience
AMERICA'S HOME PLACE, Raleigh, North Carolina   May-Aug 2005

Construction Superintendent

- Completed Superintendent Training Program
- Negotiated subcontractor prices for all trades
- Conducted pre-construction estimate reviews of projects
- Worked with County Environmental Health Depts. to obtain well & septic permits and construction authorizations
- Experienced with applying for Building Permits and working with municipalities
- Ensured Quality Control standards were met by conducting framing and foundation checks
- Evaluated lot conditions and house placement per the amount of fall on lot
- Procured building materials for each job per the established project budget
- Issued work orders to the trade contractors and adjusted prices per negotiations
- Shot existing grade on sites to determine block count for foundations
- Worked with customers to ensure a timely build out time
- Managed trade contractors on a daily basis to ensure the quality of work completed

CAROLINA SEAL & PATCH, Raleigh, North Carolina Feb-May 2002
Estimator

- Estimated for seal coating of residential and commercial parking lots
- Prepared line striping and painting estimates of parking lots
- Evaluated lots for asphalt and concrete repair
- Surveyed parking lots for new construction

Computer Skills

- AutoCAD 2000
- Expedition for Project Management
- Primavera for Project Scheduling
- Windows 2000, XP, 98
- Windows Office XP Suite

Organization Memberships

- Sigma Lambda Chi - Construction Honors Society
- East Carolina Construction Association (ECCA)
- Project Management Institute (PMI)

Functional Resume

ELANOR L. NELSON

SCHOOL ADDRESS
312 Louis St.
Greenville, NC 27858
(252) 321-9676

e1n4578@mail.ecu.edu

PERMANENT ADDRESS
11760 Black Horse Run
Raleigh, NC 27613
(919) 846-4039

Objective
An entry level position in Healthcare Marketing and Communication utilizing my skills in desk-top publishing, graphic arts, advertising and product promotions.

Marketing
DSM Pharmaceuticals, Greenville, NC,   August—Present

    Promotional Assistant (January - Present)

    Student Intern (August - December, 2003)

DSM is a leading provider of contract manufacturing to the pharmaceutical and biotechnology industries specializing in oral and topical services. I assisted in the development of marketing and product promotion materials when the company purchased Roche Vitamins, Carotinoids, and Fine Chemicals.

Healthcare
INTERIM HEALTHCARE, Greenville, NC   June—August, 2005

    Receptionist/Front Office

Interim Healthcare is a home health care service provider. I was responsible for patient scheduling, providing administrative assistance, collecting movies due, switchboard, and posting financial records.

Graphic Arts Skills
Experience in media production, communication, and illustration, including:

Layout Design	Typesetting Instructions	Printer Negotiations
Quality Control	Presentation Approaches	Illustration Creation
Esthetic Design	Production Coordination	Project Management
Strategic Planning	Dissemination Techniques	Detailed Storyboards
Concept Development	Standards and Specifications	Customer Conferencing

Computer Skills
Proficient in a variety of computer systems and software, including:

Apple Macintosh	Filemaker Pro	Pagemaker	Adobe Photoshop	FrontPage
QuarkXpress	Microsoft NT/XP	Creative Suite	Microsoft Publisher	MS Office

Education
Bachelor of Arts degree, Communications, East Carolina University   May 2006
Minor, Allied Health
G.P.A. 3.7/4.0

Selected Examples of Coursework: Public Relations, Electronic Mass Media, Audio/Video Production, Business Communications, Intercultural Communications, Advanced Writing for TV, Copy Editing and Design, Desktop Publishing, Media Sales and Promotion, and Web Design.

Professional Affiliations

Member of Alpha Epsilon Delta - Health Science Honor Society

Secretary, American Medical Student Association

Past President, Council of Pre-Health Organizations

Extra Curricular Activities

Macintosh Users Group

Member of the ECU Pirate Varsity Swim Team

Accomplishment Style Resume

ELANOR L. NELSON

SCHOOL ADDRESS		PERMANENT ADDRESS
312 Louis St.		11760 Black Horse Run
Greenville, NC 27858	eln4578@mail.ecu.edu	Raleigh, NC 27613
(252) 321-9676		(919) 846-4039

Objective . . .
An entry level position in Healthcare Marketing and Communication utilizing my skills in desk-top publishing, graphic arts, advertising and product promotions.

Capabilities Profile . . .
My proven capabilities are applicable in a variety of areas, including:

Layout Design	Typesetting Instructions	Printer Negotiations
Quality Control	Presentation Approaches	Illustration Creation
Strategic Planning	Production Coordination	Project Management
Detailed Storyboard	Dissemination Techniques	Budget Management
Marketing Strategies	Standards and Specifications	Customer Conferencing

Education . . .
Bachelor of Arts degree, Communications, East Carolina University   May 2006
Minor, Allied Health
G.P.A. 3.7/4.0

Selected Examples of Coursework: Public Relations, Electronic Mass Media, Audio/Video Production, Business Communications, Intercultural Communications, Advanced Writing for TV, Copy Editing and Design, Desktop Publishing, Media Sales and Promotion, and Web Design.

Experience . . .
DSM Pharmaceuticals, Greenville, NC,   August–Present

    Promotional Assistant (January - Present)

    Student Intern (August - December, 2003)

DSM is a leading provider of contract manufacturing to the pharmaceutical and biotechnology industries specializing in oral and topical services. I assisted in the development of marketing and product promotion materials when the company purchased Roche Vitamins, Carotinoids, and Fine Chemicals. Accomplishments Achieved:

- ✓ Designed slicks on four products which were mailed to over four thousand companies
- ✓ Developed three product advertisements which were published in regional and industry publications
- ✓ Wrote "Investors Highlights" for company annual report

Resume Continued   **ELANOR L. NELSON**   *Page Two*

(252) 321-9676

INTERIM HEALTHCARE, Greenville, NC   June–August, 2005
    Receptionist/Front Office

Interim Healthcare is a home health care service provider. I was responsible for patient scheduling, providing administrative assistance, collecting movies due, switchboard, and posting financial records. Accomplishments Achieved:

- ✓ Managed eighty patients files
- ✓ Modified all files to conform with HIPPA confidentiality regulations
- ✓ Developed computerized scheduling system which provided doctors with their daily schedule

I have a sound working knowledge of Personal Computers as well as a variety of productivity enhancing computer software packages, specifically: Macintosh and Windows operating systems, Filemaker Pro, Pagemaker, Adobe Photoshop, FrontPage, QuarkXpress, Microsoft NT/XP, Creative Suite, Microsoft Publisher, and Microsoft Word, Excel, Outlook, and PowerPoint. I have strong internet research skills.

I remain abreast of current trends within my industry and have held memberships in various professional associations, including: Member of Alpha Epsilon Delta - Health Science Honor Society, Secretary, American Medical Student Association, Past President, and Council of Pre-Health Organizations.

I am active in my community through membership in the Macintosh Users Group and as a member of the ECU Pirate Varsity Swim Team.

CREATING LETTERS THAT MARKET YOU EFFECTIVELY

A cover letter is a letter that accompanies your resume and presents the reasons why you are qualified for a specific job you are pursuing. An After Interview Letter is used to thank an employer for the interview, state why you think you are a good fit with their needs, and reaffirm your interest in the position.

Cover Letter Types

Here are some of the types of letters you might write.

Contact Letters—Sent to individuals you know from whom you want information, help, or referrals.

Referral Letters—Sent to someone you don't know to whom you have been referred because that individual either works for a company of interest or knows lots of people and may be able to help you.

Human Resources Letters—Sent to an HR department in response to a specific job opening.

Targeted Company Letters—Sent to a decision-maker at a company that interests you where you have no contacts or referrals.

While you would never send an employer an obvious form letter, certain parts of each letter type will not change from employer to employer. As you compose your letter, include those sentences or parts of sentences that are important and delete those parts which do not fit the situation. Here are some examples of letter pieces.

Letterhead

All letters will use some type of letterhead.

ELANOR L. NELSON

312 Louis St. • Greenville, NC 27858 • (252) 321-9646 • eln4578@mail.ecu.edu

Introductions

All letters will explain in the first introductory paragraph why you are writing and what you want.

For Contact Letters—As you know, I will be graduating from East Carolina University this [GRADUATION MONTH], and have begun my job search. Because I respect your opinion and judgment, I am writing to ask for your assistance. Please understand that I am not asking you for a job. I think, however, that your experience and knowledge of the current job market could prove a valuable asset in helping me explore my options.

For Referral Letters—In a recent conversation with [CONTACT], it was recommended that I contact you. [FNAME] felt that you would be a valuable resource in my job search and may be able to help me.

For Human Resource Departments—Your recent ad for a [JOB TITLE] appears to be seeking a candidate with qualities tailored to my abilities. I offer solid experience in [KEY FUNCTIONAL GROUPS RELATING TO THIS POSITION]. The enclosed resume presents my background in more depth and provides information on my capabilities.

For Targeted Company Letters—As a recognized leader in your field, [COMPANY] must be on the lookout for top talent to help the business grow. I will complete a degree in [MAJOR] this [GRADUATION MONTH] and am writing to explore the possibility that you may have need for an individual with my skills and abilities. I offer cutting edge knowledge and training in the field as well as experience in [TOP 3 FUNCTIONAL GROUPS].

Middle Paragraphs

The middle part is the crucial paragraph where you have to explain what you want. This is where you must sell yourself to the reader. If you are applying for a specific job opening, you need to address the stated requirements of the job. If you are writing directly to a decision-maker for a company that interests you, you will need to describe your areas of interest, expertise and why the employer might want to consider you.

For Contact Letters—I will graduate with a [TYPE OF DEGREE] in [MAJOR] and am interested in utilizing my skills in [TOP FOUR ACTIVITIES] to help meet the needs of companies in the private sector. I am focusing on the following industries: [TOP FOUR INDUSTRY CHOICES]. Specific companies that interest me are [LIST THE NAMES OF FOUR COMPANIES]. Please take a few minutes and look through your address book for contacts you may have who might be interested in an individual with my talents.

For Referral Letters—[CONTACT] felt that you may have an interest in a person with my experience and could be a valuable resource in my job search. I am interested in a position that would utilize my skills in [TOP 3 FUNCTIONAL GROUPS]. I have developed expertise in the areas of [THREE OR FOUR SUBJECTS YOU STUDIED] and am strong in [TECHNICAL SKILLS THAT RELATE TO THE JOB]. I recently completed an Internship/Coop experience for [ORGANIZATION] where I [ACTIVITY PROBABLY IMPORTANT TO THE READER].

For Human Resource Offices—Having carefully reviewed the stated requirements for the position, I find a close similarity between your needs and my qualifications.

Your Stated Needs	My Qualifications
(List qualifications they want that you have)	(List your corresponding education/experience, etc.)

(Listed in two columns)

For Targeted Company Letters—As a student at East Carolina University, I have been successful in [ACCOMPLISHMENT] and [ACCOMPLISHMENT]. Whether involved in [ACTIVITY], [ACTIVITY], or [ACTIVITY], I am known as a [PERSONAL MARKETING PHRASE]. I have applied my skills in [ACTIVITY] and [ACTIVITY] which resulted in [ACCOMPLISHMENT] and [ACCOMPLISHMENT] and I know that I can demonstrate the same degree of success in overcoming the challenges your company will be facing in the future.

Closing Paragraphs

The closing paragraph is used to explain what your next step will be.

For Contact Letters—If after reviewing my resume, you think of any situations where my skills and background would be a good fit, I would appreciate your comments and advice. I will call you in the near future.

For Referral Letters—Open to relocation or travel, I would welcome the opportunity to meet with you or a member of your organization to explore any available opportunities. In advance, let me thank you for your consideration. I will call in the near future.

For Human Resource Offices—My salary history has always been negotiated based upon my level of responsibility. OR (only include one of these lines if they request it in the position advertisement).

My salary requirements are flexible and negotiable and vary depending on the responsibilities of the position.

I would welcome an opportunity to meet with you and talk in more detail about my ability to contribute to your current needs. Please contact me at 252-321-9646 or by email at eln4578@mail.ecu. Thank you for your consideration.

For Targeted Company Letters—Open to relocation or travel, I would certainly welcome the opportunity to meet with you or a member of your organization to explore any available opportunities. In advance, let me thank you for your consideration. I will call in the near future.

Personal Marketing Phrases

In some of the earlier letter pieces you are asked to provide Personal Marketing Phrases. This exercise will help you identify what those might be. Please put a check mark in the box provided for those phrases which you feel would accurately describe you.

- ☐ Strong probing questioner with customer focus
- ☐ Dedicated team member who always gives 110%
- ☐ Highly effective communicator with both peers and clients
- ☐ Efficient overseer with an eye for detail
- ☐ Self-starter who enjoys a fast-paced environment
- ☐ A team-player who enjoys contributing to a goal
- ☐ Tenacious and highly energetic negotiator
- ☐ Persuasive manager who enjoys leadership
- ☐ Ambitious, with little patience for mediocrity
- ☐ Big-picture oriented and good at long-range planning
- ☐ Keen sense of timing and practical, time-saving methods
- ☐ Innate ability to prioritize needs and get things done
- ☐ Prefer harmony and a stable environment
- ☐ Constantly seeking new ways of doing things
- ☐ Workaholic, demanding high quality of self and others
- ☐ Artistic and expressive with an eye for aesthetics
- ☐ Traditional, practical and prefer working independently
- ☐ Enjoy uncovering new facts, gathering information
- ☐ A financial risk-taker who enjoys a competitive challenge
- ☐ Effective communicator with empathic sense for others
- ☐ Assertive and adventuresome offering strong leadership
- ☐ A preference for detail, accuracy, and logical expression
- ☐ Charismatic leader, able to win loyalty and get results
- ☐ Efficient perfectionist with excellent analytical skills
- ☐ Seasoned professional with an instinct for survival
- ☐ Decision-maker who stands accountable
- ☐ Dynamic strategist with an eye for marketing and profits

- ☐ Action-oriented with a focus on the bottom-line
- ☐ Unconventional and innovative
- ☐ Proactive doer and facilitator
- ☐ Analytical problem-solver
- ☐ Creative and artistic
- ☐ Keen sense of organization
- ☐ Preferring structure and systems
- ☐ Optimistic and out-going
- ☐ Self-assured and determined
- ☐ Able to bring order out of chaos
- ☐ Tough and resilient veteran of the trenches
- ☐ Empathetic and good at reading people
- ☐ Flexible and outgoing personality
- ☐ Frank and factual, and believe in straight talk
- ☐ Supportive of a strong leader
- ☐ Self-confident and persuasive
- ☐ Prefer concrete problems to ambiguous ones
- ☐ Scholarly and intellectual
- ☐ Introspective and task-oriented
- ☐ Prefer measuring results in monetary terms
- ☐ Humanistic, insightful and understanding
- ☐ Idealistic with a strong concern for others
- ☐ Strong multi-cultural orientation
- ☐ Executor of tasks with style and candor
- ☐ Operations-oriented professional
- ☐ Enthusiastic team builder
- ☐ Hands-on, shirt-sleeve manager
- ☐ Goal-oriented strategic thinker
- ☐ Strong pattern of accomplishment

From those checked, select those words or phrases which best help you compose a forceful, action-oriented description of who you are.

Copyright © Bruce Maxwell, 2004.

Complete letter examples

Here are completed examples of the four types of cover letters. Notice that in several places modifications to the letter pieces were made in order to address the specific situation and make each letter unique.

Contact Letter

ELANOR L. NELSON

312 Louis St. • Greenville, NC 27858 • (252) 321-9646 • eln4578@mail.ecu.edu

February 12, 2006

Ken Foster
4358 Eastern Pines Rd.
Greenville, NC 27834

Dear Ken,

As you know, I will be graduating from East Carolina University this May and have begun my job search. Because I respect your opinion and judgment, I am writing to ask for your assistance. Please understand that I am not asking you for a job. However, I think that your experience and knowledge of the current job market could prove a valuable asset in helping me explore my options.

I will graduate with a bachelor's degree in communication and am interested in utilizing my skills in graphic arts, advertising, product packaging, and promotion design to help meet the needs of companies in the private sector. I am focusing on the following industries: pharmaceuticals, healthcare insurance providers, medical services, and medical equipment. Some of the specific companies that interest me are Carolina Home Medical and Keen Branding in Charlotte and Aeolus Pharmaceuticals in Raleigh. Please take a few minutes and look through your address book for contacts you may have who might be interested in an individual with my talents.

If after reviewing my resume, you think of any situations where my skills and background would be a good fit, your comments and advice will be most helpful. I will call in the near future.

Sincerely,

Elanor Nelson

Enclosure: Resume

Referral Letter
Elanor L. Nelson

312 Louis St. • Greenville, NC 27858 • (252) 321-9646 • eln4578@mail.ecu.edu

February 12, 2006

John Hagans, Director of Marketing
Carolina Home Medical, Inc.
304 N. Queen St.
Goldsboro, NC 27530

Dear Mr. Hagans,

In a recent conversation with Joe Epler, he recommended that I contact you. Joe felt that you would be a valuable resource to me in my job search and may be able to help me.

I will be graduating from East Carolina University this May and with graduation rapidly approaching, I have begun a job search for a position where my skills in graphic arts, advertising, product packaging, and promotion design could be valuable to a company in the areas of pharmaceuticals, healthcare insurance providers, medical services, or medical equipment. I have two semesters of experience in Adobe Photoshop on both a Macintosh and Microsoft operating systems as well as a variety of classes in sales and marketing. For the last year I have worked for DSM Pharmaceuticals to help complete the marketing materials for a new product release. I know I can demonstrate the same degree of success for Carolina Home Medical.

I am open to regional travel and would welcome the opportunity to meet with you or a member of your organization to explore any available opportunities. In advance, let me thank you for your consideration. I will call in the near future.

Sincerely,

Elanor Nelson

Enclosure: Resume

Human Resources Letter

Elanor L. Nelson

312 Louis St. • Greenville, NC 27858 • (252) 321-9646 • eln4578@mail.ecu.edu

February 12, 2006

Human Resources
Keen Branding
310 Arlington Ave., Suite 303
Charlotte, NC 28203

Dear Sir or Madam,

Your recent ad for a Project Assistant appears to be seeking a candidate with qualities tailored to my capabilities. I offer solid experience in graphic arts, advertising, product packaging, and promotion design. My enclosed resume presents my background in more depth and provides information on my capabilities.

Having carefully reviewed the stated requirements for the position, I find a close similarity between your needs and my qualifications.

Your Stated Needs	My Qualifications
Bachelor's Degree	Bachelor's degree in Communication, May 2004
Knowledge of Adobe Photoshop	Two semester Adobe Photoshop on Mac and Windows
Strong understanding of healthcare field	Minor in healthcare
Experience in the healthcare industry	One year experience with DSM Pharmaceuticals

My salary history has always been negotiated based upon my level of responsibility. I would welcome an opportunity to meet with you and talk in more detail about my ability to contribute to your current needs. Please contact me at 252-321-9646 or by email at eln4578@a mail.ecu. Thank you for your consideration.

Sincerely,

Elanor Nelson

Enclosure: Resume

Targeted Company Letter

ELANOR L. NELSON

312 Louis St. • Greenville, NC 27858 • (252) 321-9646 • eln4578@mail.ecu.edu

February 12, 2006

Mr. Paul Grimsley, Marketing Manager
Aeolus Pharmaceuticals, Inc.
79 Tw Alexander Dr., Suite #200
Research Triangle Park, NC 27709

Dear Mr. Grimsley,

As a recognized leader in your field, Aeolus Pharmaceuticals must be on the lookout for top talent to help business grow. I will complete a bachelor's degree in communications this May and am writing to explore the possibility that you may have need for an individual with my skills and abilities. I offer cutting edge knowledge and training in the field as well as two semesters of experience in pharmaceutical promotions.

As a student at East Carolina University, I have been very successful in learning buying trends in healthcare and developing processes for assisting customers in product selection. Whether involved in developing sales brochures or composing technical descriptions, I am known as a productive and creative artist with an innate ability to prioritize needs and get things done. I have applied my skills in desktop publishing and product promotions, which resulted in my being able to convert a semester Internship into a paid position at DSM Pharmaceuticals to help develop promotions for a new product release. I know that I can demonstrate the same degree of success in overcoming the marketing challenges your company will be facing in the future.

Open to regional travel, I would certainly welcome the opportunity to meet with you or a member of your organization to explore any available opportunities. In advance, let me thank you for your consideration. I will call in the near future.

Sincerely,

Elanor Nelson

Enclosure: Resume

Answering "What Is Your Greatest Weakness?"

Ideally you want to answer every interview question in the positive. Because this question asks for negative information, it's difficult to answer correctly. Giving careful thought to your own uniqueness, you should try to come up with an answer that is both true and causes the interviewer to think well of you. Here are some examples.

1. I've been told that I set my standards for myself too high.
2. Sometimes I come on too strong with my ideas.
3. I'm something of a "workaholic" and need to develop a better balance between my commitment to the tasks I have taken on and my outside activities.
4. I've been known to get upset with others who are _____ (late to meetings, don't have their facts straight, obviously lying, lazy, take advantage of the system for their own personal gain, etc.)
5. I prefer to think of it not as an area of weakness, but as an area I am working to improve. For example, I would really like to improve my communication skills.
6. Sometimes I expect too much from those I work with.
7. I am a very detailed person and when I do problem-solving, I strive for the best answer I can find, when in fact something I come up with right away, would often work just as well.
8. Sometimes I'm impatient with people who are slow to grasp new ideas.
9. I have a strong need for organization and order. I have found that being a neat and tidy person can bother other people.
10. I'm a very creative person and sometimes others feel I'm trying to show them up when I come up with new ideas before they do.

After Interview Questionnaire

After each job interview and before you have even left the parking lot, while the details of the interview are fresh in your mind, answer these questions. (Use additional paper as necessary.)

1. How did the interview go?
2. What did you do or say that you feel went well?
3. What did you do or say that you think needs improvement or practice?

After-Interview Letters

An After-Interview Letter is sent to an employer after you have interviewed with them but before they have made a hiring decision. when you interview, keep in mind that you will be writing an After-Interview Letter and pay particular attention to the things they like about you and their needs, problems, and challenges. You will need that information when you compose this letter. Ideally you would compose the letter and post it to the mail, however, if they are likely to make the hiring decision before the mail could get to them, email the after-interview letter.

OPENING PARAGRAPH

Thank you for the opportunity to visit with you on [DAY & DATE]. I found our meeting most productive, and I appreciate being considered for a position with [COMPANY NAME].

MIDDLE PARAGRAPH

I left our meeting feeling that my background in [AREA OF EXPERTISE] with [COMPANY/CLASS] will be particularly important to your organization. In our discussion you mentioned [KEY NEED], and I enjoyed talking about [ANOTHER AREA OF PROBLEM/CHALLENGE]. As a [PERSONAL MARKETING PHRASE], I see myself as an effective [POSITION] able to [LIST TWO BENEFITS IMPORTANT TO THE INTERVIEWER]. I am anxious to become a productive member of the team and experience the fast paced environment of [COMPANY NAME].

CLOSING PARAGRAPH

I look forward to meeting with you again as we discussed on [DAY OF WEEK], [DATE], in your office. I appreciate your time and consideration.

OR

I will call on [DAY OF WEEK] of next week to discuss the next step in the hiring process. Thank you again for the courtesy extended to me.

Here is an example of a completed After-Interview Letter.

After Interview Letter
ELANOR L. NELSON

312 Louis St. • Greenville, NC 27858 • (252) 321-9646 • eln4578@mail.ecu.edu

March 12, 2006

John Hagans, Director of Marketing
Carolina Home Medical, Inc.
304 N. Queen St.
Goldsboro, NC 27530

Dear Mr. Hagans,

Thank you for the opportunity to visit with you last Wednesday, March 10, 2006. I found our meeting most productive, and I appreciate being considered for a Marketing Assistant position with Carolina Home Medical.

I left our meeting feeling that my background in product promotions with DSM Pharmaceuticals will be particularly important to your company. You mentioned the likelihood of an upcoming release of several new products, and I enjoyed our discussion of how that has caused this position to be open. I know from my own experience that having staff on hand who can respond to last minute changes in marketing materials can save thousands of dollars. As an efficient perfectionist with excellent analytical skills, I see myself as someone able to provide key quality control in this position. I am anxious to become a productive member of the team and experience the fast paced environment of Carolina Home Medical.

I will call you on Tuesday, March 16, 2006 to discuss the next step in the hiring process. I appreciate your time and consideration. Thank you again for the courtesy extended to me.

Sincerely,

Elanor L. Nelson

JOB INTERVIEWING—THE TRUE TEST OF YOUR COMMUNICATION SKILLS

No matter what company you work for, in what industry, in what position, your success depends on your ability to persuade others to your own point of view. You pitch a prospective employer to get a job. You pitch your boss to approve a project. You pitch your subordinates to live up to the spirit of your instructions, not just the letter. You pitch prospective customers to become current clients, or current customers to buy more.

One might say that every human interaction revolves around cooperation, collaboration, and persuasion. In every interaction between two humans, someone buys something. Either the prospective employer buys your employment pitch or you buy the excuses they give you. The best job interviews are not interviews at all, but more of a meeting between two professionals, discussing the needs of the company.

The job interview is your opportunity to make a pitch and sell yourself to the prospective employer. Unlike most sales situations, the prospective employer is not expecting you to have done very much to prepare yourself to pitch your product. If you allow yourself to be "cross examined," you lose much of your ability to insure a favorable outcome. You need to know how to change the dynamics of those meetings and make sure that you present yourself as well as possible.

Sometimes you are invited to an interview because there is a definite and specific position they are trying to fill, you know it, and you know what they are looking for. In other situations, they don't have a specific job opening, but more likely, you have made them curious enough to want to meet with you and explore ways in which you could be useful to their organization.

When there is a specific job opening, you have the advantage of having some specific qualifications to target and you can prepare responses to demonstrate your qualifications. Realize that they have already decided that you are qualified for the job or you wouldn't be here. Unfortunately, you are also saddled with the problem that before you meet with them their perception of the best candidate is likely to be the person with the best qualifications. You will be better off if you move the conversation away from qualifications back to needs, problems, and challenges.

When there is no job opening, but they still agree to a meeting, you have the disadvantage of not knowing what the hot buttons are which will make them hire you, often because they don't even know themselves. On the other hand, you have the advantage of not having to compete with other candidates.

In either situation, your goal for this meeting is to satisfy their concerns about your ability to do the job, but more importantly, you are here not so you can talk to them, but so *they* can talk to you. You want all decision-makers to talk about their needs, problems, and challenges. You make that happen through the questions you ask.

If there is an opening, what is the interviewer looking for? What does she really want? What type of a person will get along best with her? With this information, you will know how to make your pitch in terms that will fit this company, make them *believe* that you are giving them the best deal, and make them *feel* good about hiring you.

In the situation where you go to a problem-solving meeting, the goal is to identify, or help them identify their perception of their problems in your area of expertise. You do this by asking probing, problem-focused questions.

Most job interviewers worry about knowing the "right" answers to the questions they will be asked and they spend hours searching through self-help job interviewing books for new questions they have never seen. I submit that it is not *what* you say that is the most important; it is how what you say is *perceived*. The most critical skill is not your ability to come up with successful answers to their questions, it is your ability to actively listen to how those answers are perceived and to overcome the obstacles the interviewers present. Remember, this is sales. Once you have identified their obstacles, you are halfway there!

Be prepared to provide effective stories which demonstrate your ability to help solve the problems identified, but don't actually provide solutions to their problems. If you tell them in the interview what they can do to solve the problems, why should they hire you? If you are willing to give it away for free, why should they pay you for it? You are *not* there to solve their problems, but to identify those problems and make them believe you can help them solve these problems by demonstrating your expertise in this area.

Think of this event not as an interview, but as a meeting. A first interview with a decision-maker typically has four parts:

1. Developing rapport;
2. They ask you questions;
3. They tell you about the job/tasks they have in mind;
4. They give you a chance to ask questions and talk about the next step in the hiring process.

But that is *their* agenda. It differs in small but significant ways from *your* agenda, which is:

1. Developing rapport;
2. Probing into their needs by working into the conversation your own questions;
3. Presenting your skills, abilities, and experience in a way that will address the needs you uncover;
4. Identifying the obstacles to hiring you and overcoming them.
5. Securing a job offer or a second interview.

When encouraging the conversation to follow your agenda, it is not unusual for the interviewer to set aside their preplanned list of questions and get into a real discussion about the needs they have.

Preparing for the Interview

Before you go on an interview, you will need to research the interviewer, the department, the company, and the industry. So much information is available today on the internet, that the first place to go is the company's own web site. Follow each link on the site to see where it goes. Print off anything that interests you. Find their internal search engine. Enter the name(s) of the interviewer, the department, their products or services, the name of the president of the company, key words like annual meeting, prospectus (if they are publicly traded), customer service, public relations, whatever you can think of. Print off everything, because until you have it all, you won't see the connections between items you read. Next you need to research the industry. Some web sites to use include:

http://stats.bls.gov/oco/cg/home.htm,
http://www.hoovers.com/free/,
http://company.monster.com/
http://home.sprintmail.com/~debflanagan/,
http://bwnt.businessweek.com/company/search.asp
http://www.washingtonpost.com/wp-dyn/business/companyresearch/
http://www.quintcareers.com/researching_companies.html

When you begin to run out of places to look, sit down and read through it all. Sort the sheets into piles of similar information. Next highlight the key points on each sheet. Transfer and consolidate all the key points onto sheets of paper by topic. What additional questions does this uncover? What are the key problems of the industry? The company? The department? Prepare open-ended questions that probe into these problem areas. Write them on the back of a 3x5 index card. Make up a second card with the key information you find out in your research and bring it with you.

Dress

The standard rule of thumb for work attire is to dress for the job you want, not the job you have. Your goal is to fit in, but still look like you are dressed up. So dress the way the people there will dress, except dress just a little better. If the men wear collared shirts, wear a tie (but not a suit). If the mean wear suits, wear a dark grey or navy blue suit with a white starched shirt and tie. If the women wear suits, wear a gray or navy blue suit with a white blouse and accessories. On the other hand, if the women who work there wear blue jeans and you show up in a suit, you're over-dressed and won't fit in. The best way to find out what you should wear is to go to the company and see what the employees in your area wear at work. If you live in the same city, you can do that by going a week or so early and asking for a tour of the facility. This has the added advantage of allowing you to find the place before the day of the interview so you won't be late. Tell the tour guide what department you want to make sure to visit. Look at what the people who work there are wearing.

For the Interview

Preparation is the key to a good interview. Do everything you can to reduce your anxiety. Drive by the interview location a couple of days ahead of time so you can work out how to get there. On the day of the interview, arrive ten minutes early. If you get there before that, sit out in the car and wait. You don't want to appear over-anxious. Walk up to the receptionist and tell her/him, "Hello, My name is _____ and I am here for an interview with _____. Do you happen to have some literature on the company I could read while I wait?" Now read it. You will find nine times out of ten that whatever they hand you will have information that will turn out to be useful in the interview.

Making a Good First Impression

There are five specific things you need to do in order to insure a good first impression:

1. Smile (show your teeth). Interviewing is hard work and you need to make it look easy.
2. Make direct eye contact. Even if you are interviewing with a committee, always look people in the eye. Pretend you are having a conversation with one or more members of your audience, then look at them and talk to them. Don't look at their mouths, or their chests, or their hair. Look only in their eyes and don't look away more than 50% of the time even if this is uncomfortable and not what you would normally do.
3. Know and use their name. Call the day beforehand to confirm the appointment. Speak to the secretary and say, "Hello, this is _____, I am calling to confirm my 10 o'clock appointment with _____. Can you please tell me who will be attending besides _____?" If there is anyone else, get his/her name, title, and role in the company. Then research that person as well. You will be amazed how often the secretary will give you this information, because so rarely does anyone ask this question, that no one will have told him or her not to give the information to you. In addition, if for some reason the meeting has been changed in some way, you will be informed.
4. Be the first person to extend your hand to be shaken and match their style of hand shake. You are demonstrating how well you fit in, so regardless of how the person shakes your hand, **match that style**.
5. Give a Power Greeting!

Develop a Power Greeting

Throughout your job search and especially when you are in a job interview, you need to be able to introduce yourself in a powerful way to people who don't know you. What you say at that moment will set the tone for the rest of your interaction. To do this most effectively, you need a power greeting.

A power greeting is like a "30-second commercial." It provides just enough information to make the listener want to know more about you and sets a professional tone for the rest of your interaction.

It is clearly in your best interest to control this introduction and advance preparation is the key. A power greeting is composed of three distinct parts and a follow-up question:

1. Your education and credentials (what you have studied?)
2. Your experience in the field (employment, internship/COOP, volunteer positions)
3. Your strengths (what you do best?)
4. An open-ended probing question about their needs, problems, and challenges.

Here's an example, "Let me tell you about myself, I hold a Bachelor's degree in Industrial Technology from East Carolina University with a minor in Business Administration. I have a year and a half experience in the field through a Summer Internship with NACCO Material Handling Group in Greenville, NC, and a two semester COOP position with National Waterworks in Charlotte, NC. I have discovered that I enjoy supply chain management and Just-in-Time delivery challenges. I chose this field because I enjoy finding new ways of solving problems, I am a hands-on person, and I like getting into the thick of things and dealing with tangible, concrete problems. What role does logistics play in your business?

Your Turn

Let me tell you about myself, I hold a _____ degree in _____

from east Carolina University (is your minor in _____ related?). I have

_____ experience in the field through _____

_____.

I have discovered that I enjoy _____

I chose this field because _____

_____

Now ask your first question, even if they told you to hold your questions until later:

Is there anything in particular you would like to know about me?

These five things need to be repeated at the close of the meeting as well. The interview is over, you walk to the door of their office, stop at the doorway (or at the exit door to the building or wherever the parting moment will occur) and, repeat these same five steps: smile, direct eye contact, use their name, and shake hands, and give them a power close—based on what you've learned during the interview, tell them why they should hire you. Do it! These five steps will double the number of offers you receive.

Controlling the Environment

Where you physically position yourself during the interview is an important variable in effective interviewing. When you walk into the interview room you have options. Take control to improve the likelihood of a successful interview, by controlling to the extent you can—how and where you sit. As they motion for you to enter the room, decide where it is most advantageous for you to sit. Sometimes there are no options. The decision-maker has his desk and one chair sitting on the other side. In that case, correct the position of the chair if necessary and sit directly across from the interviewer so that your shoulders are parallel to his/her shoulders.

Occasionally, there will be a coffee table and set of chairs off to the side. If possible, get the interviewer out from behind his/her desk (and position of power) to join you in conversation as peers at the chairs off to the side. You make this happen by not waiting for the decision-maker to tell you where to sit, and moving directly to stand by one of the two chairs off to the side. This way the decision-maker will tell you to have a seat and will come sit in the other chair with you.

When faced with an interview in a board or conference room, you choose a seat on the opposite side of the room from the door, at one end of the table (but not the very end, if possible). As you enter the room you would move to that chair and stand there until asked to be seated. When interviewing for a panel, you want to position yourself squarely in the center facing the panel members. Turn your upper torso and head to face the individuals as they speak to you.

Communication is composed of three parts, the words you say, the way you use your voice (vocal inflection), and the way your body communicates how you feel (non-verbals). Research in this field has shown that 60% of our communication is non-verbal. We all communicate at two levels, a conscious, intentional level, and an unconscious, unintentional level. Yet of the two, the unconscious, unintentional communication between two people is considered by communication specialist as the more accurate of the two. Ask yourself, how long after you come home at night does it take you to know if your roommate has had a bad day? Or how long does it take you to know if your mother is angry with you in some way? Rarely does either person have to actually SAY anything at all. Their non-verbal communication speaks out loud and clear. You want to position yourself so that you can read their non-verbals and you want to control as much as possible your non-verbals so your body communicates the right message.

There are five additional key environmental considerations and the acronym SOLER is used to help you remember them:

SOLER

S—Straight Since your unconscious communication processes are most effective face-to-face you will do the best job of interpreting the non-verbal communication of the interviewer if you are facing him or her. Sit straight in front of the person you are interviewing so that your shoulders are parallel to his of her shoulders (even if you have to move the chair slightly or sit slightly crooked to do so).

O—Open Control your non-verbals and make sure that you send open, receptive non-verbal messages. No folding of arms or legs (keep your feet on the ground). No playing with objects (pencils, buttons, purse straps, etc.). Be pleasant, smile often, and be open.

L—Lean Decision-makers like to see that others respect them. One way to convey respect, is to lean slightly forward when THEY are talking (and sit up straight when you are talking), as if what they are saying is the most important and interesting thing you have heard all day.

E—Eye Contact Most people have direct eye contact about 50% of the time when they are talking, but about 80% of the time when they are listening. Decision-makers expect you to be providing good eye contact when they are talking. You are not (and should not) expected to maintain 100% eye contact 100% of the time when you are talking.

R—Relax It is your responsibility to put the interviewer at ease. You can't do that when you are nervous. Relax. If you have nervous energy, practice clenching and unclenching the toes of each foot, right-left, right-left.

Learn from Your Mistakes

If your sole criterion for evaluating your effectiveness as an interviewer is whether or not you get a specific offer, then you are likely to experience considerable disappointment. After all, there is always a great deal of rejection in sales, because you don't have all that much control. Sometimes, in spite of all your preparation, and for reasons beyond your control, people don't buy. However, if you set as a goal the objective of making each interview the best one you have ever done and you strive to get several interviews for different jobs, you will find yourself with multiple job offers and real control over your future. Concentrate not on simply getting through this interview, but on improving your interview skills every time.

It is not unusual for you to be blocked mentally, and suddenly not be able to remember any of the questions or stories you prepared. At a time like that, it is a good idea to have notes available. But instead of a notebook with a pad of paper, use 3x5 cards that will easily fit in your pocket or purse. Take one card and on one side put the names of all your stories. On the other side, write the key questions that you need to cover and then secondary topics that might lead to a useful discussion.

Sentence Completion Exercise

Most students lack sufficient work experience to qualify outright for the jobs they are pursuing. Therefore it becomes critical that you learn how to communicate your potential. You go to school to gain knowledge and develop skills through coursework, Internships, class projects, and homework. We know that the best predictor of future performance is past behavior, which tells us that sharing examples of your related school work is an effective job search tool. The tendency is however, to downplay the significance of those projects because we didn't get paid to do them. We often fail to recognize them as significant accomplishments worthy of being mentioned. After all, these projects are tangible evidence that you are a qualified, effective worker who is able to utilize particular skills to produce results.

A story is an excellent way to demonstrate our potential, but it is really hard to come up with stories to tell. Please complete as many of the following sentence fragments as you can. Quantify your examples using dollars, time, percentages, of increase or decrease, or cost reductions, as much as possible. From these examples you will be able to create stories to tell employers.

In School

1. One project I did in school that I felt really good about was

    _____

    _____

2. One time that I went beyond what was asked of me by the professor was

    _____

    _____

3. One group project where I ended up doing most of the work was

_____

_____

4. One homework assignment in my major I really enjoyed was

_____

_____

5. One project I did for extra credit was

_____

_____

6. One time the teacher told the whole class about my project was when

_____

_____

7. One time I got an "A" on an assignment that surprised me was

_____

_____

8. One time I won an award in school was for

_____

_____

9. One time my grade on a project was near the top of the class was when

_____

_____

10. One time the teacher complemented my work was

_____

_____

11. One time I helped someone else in my class by

_____

_____

On an Internship/Job

12. One time I solved a problem was when

_____

_____

13. One time I reduced complaints by

_____

_____

14. One thing I did at work that I felt really good about was

_____

_____

15. One time I reorganized a mess when

_____

_____

16. One time when I was able to do more with less was

_____

_____

17. One time I improved a process or procedure that

_____

_____

18. One good thing my boss said in a performance review was

_____

_____

19. One time I went beyond what was required to just do the job by

_____

_____

20. One good thing my boss said about me was

_____

_____

21. One time I dealt with an angry customer/client/co-worker by

_____

_____

22. One time I streamlined a program/project/operation by

_____

_____

23. One time I received a compliment or award for

_____

_____

24. One time I made a customer happy by

_____

_____

25. One time I saved the company money by

_____

_____

26. One time I made the company money when

_____

_____

27. One time I coordinated a project with

_____

_____

COMMUNICATING EFFECTIVELY USING STORIES—SACS

We live in a story-based society. Our society uses stories to communicate importance, meaning and values. Urban legends, for example, are stories filled with subtle meaning used by members of society to pass on to others the rules whereby we live. Parents have utilized stories for generations to pass on values to their children. They frequently gossip about neighbors' problems and use those stories to pass on to their children their understanding of how to live successfully and effectively within our society.

Over the generations of story-telling, we have developed an almost innate ability to decipher stories. This becomes important to the job seeker because it makes stories an effective job search tool. The job seeker tells a story and decision-makers use their own ability to draw meaning from that story to interpret the job seeker's potential as a problem-solver.

Copyright © Bruce Maxwell, 2004.

Job seekers are trying to demonstrate to others that they will be high performers in the future and valuable employees. The best way to do that is to tell stories of past situations where they were high performers and where their efforts made a difference.

Unfortunately, American society has complicated matters by also teaching us that it is inappropriate to brag about ourselves and aggrandize our accomplishments. As a result, when we do a good job of overcoming an obstacle, the tendency is to downplay the significance of our efforts and depreciate our worth. Instead we live by the philosophy that we should let our actions show what type of people we are and we leave it up to others to tell stories about us. As a result of this societal training, we have real difficulty coming up with stories about our accomplishments and in fact we rarely acknowledge to ourselves that we even made a difference.

This is where the acronym SAC becomes a useful tool to the job seeker. When you are telling a SAC story, you are not bragging, you are simply telling a factual story. We need a way to present our stories in a short and concise manner fitting the time limitations of an interaction with a potential employer, yet one which will also do job of communicating our potential.

SAC stands for:
Situation
Action
Consequence

Review the sentence completion exercise you just completed. Identify the accomplishments which are most closely related to the work you will do in this career. Use the SAC form on the following page to develop at least TEN stones about events/exercises/volunteer and work experiences before your interview. Photocopy this next page and write one story on each page.

SAC Stories

TITLE_____

SITUATION:

(Describe the project, assignment, condition, situation, need, problem, or challenge presented by this story.)

ACTION:

(What did you personally do to correct the problem, resolve the situation, or take advantage of an opportunity?)

CONSEQUENCE:

(What were the results of your actions? Quantify the benefit wherever possible by presenting the result in a percentage comparisons, dollars, decreases, increases, reductions, time, numbers of people or products, etc.)

QUESTION:

Pick a topic covered by your SAC and ask an open-ended question about that topic to help you learn additional information.

_____

Copyright © Bruce Maxwell, 2004.

GENERATING QUESTIONS TO ASK

Questions help you learn about available jobs and the companies themselves. Some job seekers seem to learn more and get farther in the interview faster than others. If you were to tape record the conversations of effective job seekers and analyze those conversations, you would find that the types of questions being asked are formed differently and cause company representatives to do more of the talking and reveal more important information. The most effective questions are ones that focus on the company's needs, problems and challenges. Sometimes you find out that they are not even aware that these issues are problems. Often you find that they are not devoting the time, energy, and resources to solving the problem. But the crucial motivator is when you help them begin to realize what the costs are for not solving these problems now. That is when they will hire you. Our goal in this lesson is to teach you the secrets of asking questions that focus on the needs, problems, and challenges of the organization so you can become an expert at asking questions.

Question Composition

Questions are either open or closed. Closed questions are ones that can be answered with a yes or no, or request specific information. Open questions cannot be answered by yes or no and force the speaker to talk about a subject.

CLOSED questions often begin with:

Are	Did
Do	Would
Can	Is
Does	Which

OPEN questions begin with:

Who	At what time
What	Tell me about
When	In what way
Where	In which way
Why	Describe
How	To what extent

After all, the company will not hire you because you are a nice person. They will not hire you because they like your resume. Only if the company has or anticipates having a problem that must be solved and you are able to demonstrate that you have the ability to solve that problem, will they hire you. The difficulty job seekers face is how to identify those problems. As a job seeker, you don't know what it is that you don't know and you must ask open-ended questions that bring out into the open what problems the company is having in your area of expertise. You are trying to get them to identify what those pivotal needs, problems and challenges are. To do that, you must asked open-ended, fact-finding questions.

Sample Probing Questions

Here are examples of questions that may be useful to you as you prepare questions for companies you are interviewing. Identify about ten questions you like the best. Write them on a 3x5 card and take them to the interview with you.

1. What areas of the company do you believe offer the greatest opportunity for growth?
2. How has the growth of your company made it difficult to get tasks completed?
3. What is your current rate of turnover in this department?
4. To what extent has the rate of employee turnover caused problems for you?
5. How well do you feel your company is meeting customer needs?
6. What issues are you currently facing with staff productivity?
7. What are some of the services you'd like to offer customers, but can't right now?
8. How do you collect information on quality control efforts?
9. What programs or services are not cost-effective? Why?
10. What would you like to see employees do differently to save you money and improve profits?
11. How do you stay current on new developments in the field?
12. How do the results of this department affect the rest of the company?
13. What are the most difficult projects the company is currently working on?
14. How does your company compare to that of your competitors?
15. What are your goals for the future of the company?
16. How well do your current employees work together?
17. What types of problems/situations give the company the most trouble?
18. What would be the most difficult problem I would face if you offered me this job?
19. Tell me about the last time the company had to choose between producing a quality service and meeting a deadline.
20. Tell me about a current project where the company had to overcome major obstacles to get it completed.
21. What types of situations cause your employees the greatest amount of stress?

Screening-Out Interview Questions

Instructions: Please write out an answer for each question as you would in an interview. Use additional paper as necessary. (Hint: Look for opportunities to tell stories.)

1. Tell me about yourself. (Hint: Use your power greeting)

2. What do you know about our organization?

3. What are your qualifications for this position?

4. Tell me about a team project of which you are particularly proud of your contribution.

5. What aspects of this position interest you the most?

6. Why should we hire you?

7. What are your short and long term career goals? (Short-term is to make this transition, get into this field, get this job. Long-term is to be an effective leader/manager and make a difference)

8. What are your greatest strengths?

9. What is your greatest weakness?

10. Tell me about your experience in school.

11. What are your salary requirements?

12. What else do you think I should know about you?

Plan what you will say and how you will say it. Develop convincing rebuttals to possible objections. Remember, the employer *expects* to have to bargain. Your job is to convince him or her that what you bring to the relationship is valuable and should be compensated accordingly.

Improve your delivery by practicing with your roommate, your girlfriend, your spouse, or even a tape recorder.

Timing

There are three phases of salary negotiations.

First Phase

Whoever names a salary figure first loses, so discuss salary only *after* you have been offered the job, in all other cases dodge the topic.

In the initial screening process, they will ask: "what are your salary requirements?"

You respond, "In the past I have always been paid according to the responsibilities of the position. I really don't know enough about this position to say Tell me, what did you like best about the performance of the person who held this position last?" (Distract them with a question).

Second Phase

After rapport and interest has been established, but before they are convinced that you are the right person for the job, they ask: "What salary are you expecting?"

You respond, "what salary range have you budgeted for the position?" Once they give you a range, you can position yourself in the top half of that range. They say, "The range is $35-45,000." You say, "well that's about what I had in mind, but I see myself between $40-50,000."

Once they understand what it will take to get you, they won't pursue it any further until they are ready to make an offer. If they continue to pursue a specific figure say, "Does this mean that you are prepared to make me an offer?"

Third Phase

Once they have made you an actual offer, you begin the process of negotiating first the salary, then the benefits.

If they offer you the job *without* talking about salary and benefits, you say. "I am thrilled to hear that you want to hire me. What is the offer you are making?"

Negotiate benefits only after your salary has been agreed upon.

Set realistic, achievable salary and benefit goals. Remember, pigs get fatter, hogs get slaughtered.

Be prepared to ask for "disposables," items that you are willing to throw away so you will be appearing to make concessions. Read through this list and prioritize them in terms of their importance to you. If you don't ask, you won't receive.

Fringe Benefits

Sales Commissions
Equity Position
Disability Insurance
Paid Sick Leave
Profit Sharing
Outplacement
Mortgage Funds
Short-Term Loan
Company Car
Season Tickets (i.e. opera, professional sports)
Bonus
Health Insurance
Dental Insurance
Personal Days
Vacation Length
Expense Account
Company Services
Executive Dining Privileges
Membership (i.e., country club)
Matching Employer Retirement Contributions (401K)
Stock Options
Life Insurance
Optical Insurance
Retirement Annuity
Pre-Defined Severance Pay
Tuition Reimbursement
Start Date
Compensatory Time

HAVE A POSITIVE ATTITUDE

Remember, the company would never have made an offer if they didn't want you and that they tend to put a higher value on something if they have to pay a higher price for it.

When you feel you have the least leverage to negotiate, is when you must demonstrate the most self-confidence. If you cannot communicate a fundamental regard for yourself and your skills, then successful negotiations will elude you.

Contrary to public belief, standing up for yourself does not threaten,the likelihood of the company hiring you, it *strengthens* it. Employers quickly conclude that confident negotiators, who can look out for their own interests, are probably better equipped to look out for the company's interests as well.

You may feel that you cannot afford to negotiate, when in fact, you cannot afford *not* to negotiate. If you don't place a high worth on your skills and talents, neither will the employer and vice versa.

Do's and Don'ts

1. DON'T be the first to mention a figure or a range.
2. DO know what you are worth.
3. DON'T accept an offer at the time it is made.
4. DON'T be afraid to ask for more time to make the best decision (especially if you have other options).
5. DON'T accept any counter offers from your current employer. Forget it and move on (More than 50% of all employees who accept counter offers change companies within the following 24 months).
6. DO sidestep the money question until you know the employer is definitely interested in you.
7. DO negotiate an early salary and performance review regardless of what they offer you.
8. DO negotiate only with the decision-maker.
9. DON'T start negotiating until *after* you have received an offer.
10. DO write a thank you letter immediately after your interview and *mail* it. Don't email the letter unless they will make a decision before the letter could reach them.

If the salary and benefits you are asking for are realistic, approach the negotiation with a cooperative and friendly, but persistent attitude. If you have effectively presented what you can do to make a difference within their organization, they will hire you.

REVIEW OF COMMUNICATION TOOLS ESSENTIAL TO WINNING THE JOB

When you stop to consider that the average student will spend the next 40 years of their life in a career, managing that transition from school to your first career position is critical. The communication tools you learn in this course will turn out to be some of the most important lessons you will ever have in school because they are crucial you your success in life. This chapter presented you with a variety of communication tools that will increase your effectiveness as a job seeker and improve your success at getting into your career of choice.

In this chapter you learned:

1. The job search process
2. That resumes and cover letters need to be written so that they market you to meet the needs of employers
3. Where to go to find out what an employer need and would hire you to do
4. How to determine what type of resume you should create
5. How to write the different types of job search letter you will need
6. The dynamics of the job interview
7. How to prepare for a job interview
8. Your accomplishments and how to use them to sell your potential
9. How to write SAC stories
10. How to ask open-ended probing questions
11. How to negotiate salary and benefits

Communication is the basis for each of these lessons. Communication is a learned skill and only through your efforts to communicate effectively will you develop the skills you need to be who you want to be in life.

Group Work

ONE GROUP WORK ASSIGNMENT (4 GROUPS)

Goal:

For this group project you will be teaching your fellow classmates about what group work is and how to perform well in a group. You will work together to develop a presentation for the class that demonstrates positive group work. You will learn about different aspects of group work and how to perform well as a unit.

Assignment:

Each group will be assigned a particular part of a chapter to teach the class. All of the units are concerning group work and how to achieve a task as a team. You will prepare a 20-25 minute presentation in which you will teach the class about your particular assigned topic. These topics will not be covered in class; it's your group's responsibility to teach the class the material you are designated to cover. Every group member will participate in the presentation. **Due Date** _____

Topics

1. Defining groups and member roles

   - define groups
   - norms, cohesiveness
   - types of roles

2. Thinking about how groups function

   - conformity
   - group think
   - advocacy
   - do not cover conflict

3. Aggressiveness, bargaining, and negotiating

   - argumentative and verbal aggressiveness
   - strategic bargaining
   - negotiating

4. Group conflict
    - conflict
    - conflict styles and tactics
    - communication competence
    - goal setting

Requirements:

Have fun and be CREATIVE!!!

- Prepare a 20-25 minute presentation thoroughly covering your topic, (Remember 20-25 minutes is not that long. You want to pick out the most important information.)
- Every group member must participate in presentation.
- Visual aid required.
- Interactive activity required (skit, crossword puzzle for class, game, movie clip, etc.)

If you show a movie clip you must somehow make this activity interactive with entire class.

PEER GROUP EVALUATION

Your Name_____ Group Member_____

Strongly Agree=5, Agree=4, Unknown=3, Disagree=2, Strongly Disagree=1

This group member was faithful to outside group meetings by making every effort to attend____

This group member provided input and helped actively develop presentation and materials _____

This group member actively participated in decision making_____

This group member listened to others' ideas_____

I would enjoy working with this group member again if the opportunity arose_____

Your Name_____ Group Member_____

Strongly Agree=5, Agree=4, Unknown=3, Disagree=2, Strongly Disagree=1

This group member was faithful to outside group meetings by making every effort to attend____

This group member provided input and helped actively develop presentation and materials _____

This group member actively participated in decision making_____

This group member listened to others' ideas_____

I would enjoy working with this group member again if the opportunity arose_____

Your Name_____ Group Member_____

Strongly Agree=5, Agree=4, Unknown=3, Disagree=2, Strongly Disagree=1

This group member was faithful to outside group meetings by making every effort to attend____

This group member provided input and helped actively develop presentation and materials _____

This group member actively participated in decision making_____

This group member listened to others' ideas_____

I would enjoy working with this group member again if the opportunity arose_____

Your Name_____ Group Member_____

Strongly Agree=5, Agree=4, Unknown=3, Disagree=2, Strongly Disagree=1

This group member was faithful to outside group meetings by making every effort to attend____

This group member provided input and helped actively develop presentation and materials _____

This group member actively participated in decision making_____

This group member listened to others' ideas_____

I would enjoy working with this group member again if the opportunity arose_____

PEER EVALUATION FORM

Instruction: Evaluate each member of your group (excluding yourself) in the following five categories in light of the descriptive criteria.

FIVE CRITERIA	DESCRIPTION OF WORK
1. Time Commitment	This person attended meetings, arrived on time, stayed the entire time to work on the group project, and made effort to contribute one's time in some way even if it was difficult.
2. Output Quantity	This person offered enough amount of input to the group project, by providing creative ideas, information, skills, and critical thinking.
3. Output Quality	This person took this project seriously and offered high-quality information, ideas, and skills needed for the task to be completed, instead of joking around.
4. Communication	This person was approachable and available for group work, and used affirmative and constructive communication to build positive and supportive climate of a group.
5. Cooperation/Respect	This person treated each group member equally with respect and works cooperatively as a team member without disrupting the process of group work.

Please evaluate each team member according to these criteria listed above using the following scale:

    1 = Unacceptable, 2 = Poor, 3 = Acceptable, 4 = Good, 5 = Outstanding

Group #_____ Your Name_____

Member Name					
1. Time Commitment					
2. Output Quantity					
3. Output Quality					
4. Communication					
5. Cooperation Respect					
Total Points					
General Comments (any Feedback about this person's participation to the group project)					

Managing Anxiety

Everybody gets nervous when they have to speak in public. The trick is to NOT let the fear overwhelm you. Prepare carefully, practice your speech out loud many times with a stop watch handy, refine, then practice again.

On the day of your speech, write out a checklist. Do you have your outline with works cited page, notecards, VHS-C tape, visual aid, and are you dressed professionally?

Try to exercise in the morning if you have some extra time. An aerobics class, a brisk walk or jog or weightlifting would be ideal! No time? How about walking to class instead of catching a ride with a friend? Impossible? Okay, climb the stairs to class . . . several times! Anything you can do to burn that excess energy will help calm the butterflies and make the nervousness subside. Try to eat a light breakfast, or if you just can't stomach food early in the day, at least drink a glass of juice.

Double-check your back pack to make sure you have everything you need. Then, just as you walk out of the house check it again.

Finally, take a deep breath and think positively!

CHANGING COGNITION

Roller Coaster Example

We all engage in an internal dialogue with ourselves, which serves the double function of shaping our view of the world and then allowing us to express that view. It's often referred to as "self talk". This is very different from "talking to yourself" out loud which will get you strange looks if you do it too much.

Let me give you an example.

Two friends ride on a roller coaster together. As they exit the ride, one says, "That was awesome!!" The other one comments, "That was awful." Their self talk probably went something like this:

I think I'm going to die.	This is so much fun.
I'm really scared.	This is scary but I know there are safety precautions to protect me.
This is never going to end.	The ride lasts only a few minutes.
I cant stand this.	This is the nearest thing to flying.
I'm going to be sick.	I can close my eyes if I need to.
I have to get off now.	I have a friend right beside me
I'm never going to do this again.	I've done it!

Center for Counseling and Student Development, ECU.

Which one is right?

The answer is, of course, both. They did have the same experiences but their internal "self talk" influenced their perception of it.

The point of all this is if self talk does determine how we perceive a situation which in turn affects how we react to it, then IT IS POSSIBLE TO PURPOSEFULLY USE SELF TALK WHICH CREATES A POSITIVE PERCEPTION WHICH REDUCES THE NEGATIVE REACTION. This idea is frequently referred to as cognitive restructuring.

We're going to take a little different approach.

THE CYCLE OF SPEECH ANXIETY

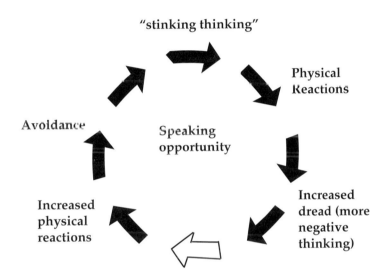

Speech anxiety is part of a cycle. We'll be talking about all of the items in the cycle except one and it is potentially the most dangerous.

Is it our physical reaction? No, there are no verified reports of anyone actually perishing from speech anxiety.

Is it our negative thoughts ("stinking thinking")? No, negative thoughts are powerful but we'll talk about how to change those.

The answer—avoidance. Speech anxiety causes people to avoid the one thing that can help them the most—experience.

- Some people avoid certain jobs if they involve public speaking.
- Others turn down promotions which require giving presentations.
- Believe it or not, students have been known to choose their majors based on whether or not a course in public speaking is required.

EXAMPLES OF STINKING THINKING

The human mind is very powerful!! We've already talked about our ability to shape experiences by our attitude toward them. Our negative thoughts about giving a speech are represented by the term **"stinking thinking"** in our cycle of speech anxiety.

What are the thoughts or feelings you experience in a public speaking situation?

Take a moment to think about what you might experience when you're given a speaking assignment or when you're sitting there just prior to giving a speech.

We've tried to help you out by including a list of 21 of the thoughts that commonly occur to people in that situation. Read over the list and put a check by the ones with which you can identify.

- ☐ What if they're not interested in what I have to say?
- ☐ I wish I had practiced (or prepared) more.
- ☐ They're going to see that my hands (or knees) are shaking.
- ☐ I'm afraid I'll forget something or my mind will go blank.
- ☐ Everyone else will do better than me.
- ☐ My heart is pounding so loud I know everyone can hear it.
- ☐ What if I really mess up in front of these people I have to be with for the rest of the semester?
- ☐ Do I know what I'm talking about?
- ☐ How can I get out of this?
- ☐ It seems like I can't get enough air.
- ☐ I hate giving speeches.
- ☐ How can I make them understand me?
- ☐ I'm going to sound stupid.
- ☐ I've got to get and A (or pass or get a good grade).
- ☐ I know I am going to talk too fast.
- ☐ My stomach doesn't feel so good.
- ☐ I'm no good at this. I can't do this.
- ☐ I don't know how to begin.
- ☐ I think I'm going to faint.
- ☐ People will laugh or think less of me if I mess up.
- ☐ If I don't look at them, I can pretend they're not there.

Now go back through and select your "top five" list. Select five that occur to you most often or are the most troubling to you. These should also be items that represent something that you really feel might actually happen.

We've only asked you to select five to give us a focus for out work. Also, this is only one short speech and ALL of the things on your list could not possibly happen in one speech!

List your top five on a sheet of paper.

1. _____

2. _____

3. _____

4. _____

5. _____

Mental Magnets—Replaces Top Five Negative Thoughts with Positive Thoughts

If you've ever played with or used a magnet, then you know how they latch onto a metal object whenever they get close to it. And they stick there.

What we're going to develop is a list of "Mental Magnets" which are positive statements, which can latch onto the negative thoughts from your "Top Five" list whenever you use them.

Based on approximately 2,000 years of studying and teaching public speaking (Aristotle and Plato made their living as speech teachers), There are some things we know to be pretty true:

- No audience is as aware of my nervousness as I am.
- Most of the time people don't notice my little mistakes as much as I do.
- Public speaking is a skill. If I follow the step-by-step process, I can do this.
- No one can give a perfect speech.
- Everyone experiences some nervousness before giving a speech.
- Just because I'm nervous doesn't mean I can't give a good speech.
- A few mistakes will not ruin my speech.
- These people can benefit from what I have to share with them.
- I have done the best I can to prepare for this speech.
- Even if I make a mistake, I can learn from it and improve the next time.
- The audience knows how I feel and is rooting for me.

- ◆ I talk to people all day long. This kind of speaking is not that different.
- ◆ The world will not end even if I really mess up.

With your "top five" list in hand, look over the above list. Find statements, which seem to be the opposite of your negative thoughts. These will be your "mental magnets" which will latch on to your negative thoughts whenever they appear!

PHYSICAL TOOLS FOR MANAGING SPEECH ANXIETY

These tools might be useful at several points in the preparation process:

- ◆ *To relax you so that you can concentrate on thorough preparation*
- ◆ *To help you create a positive image in your mind before the speaking situation*
- ◆ *To calm last-minute jitters the day of the speech*
- ◆ *To adapt to physical reactions during the speech.*

Our major tools will be:

1. Muscular Relaxation
2. Abdominal Breathing
3. Physical Exercise

Muscular Relaxation

Our knowledge of the human body indicates that we can not experience two opposite states at the same time. Tension and relaxation are opposite states so we can use one to substitute for the other.

Try this with your fist. Begin by resting it on the table in front of you. Make a fist as tight as you can. Hold it for five seconds and then release. Notice the contrast. Let the warmth and relaxation flow into it, If you try this three times in a row, you will notice that the relaxation is there to stay.

The extreme tensing allows the muscles to reach a higher state of relaxation after the tension is released.

This same kind of relaxation can be achieved especially in your legs and hands (which tend to give us trouble by trembling). This exercise can be done in ways that will not be noticed even by the person sitting next to you by:

- ◆ pressing your toes against the floor as hard as you can. Hold. Release. Repeat three times.
- ◆ pointing your toes to the ceiling. Hold. Release. Repeat three times.

- pressing you hands together until your forearms are tight. Hold. Release. Repeat three times.
- making a fist. Hold. Release. Repeat three times.
- pressing the side of your foot against the leg of your chair. Hold. Release. Repeat three times.

Use all of these for general bodily relaxation or just the ones you need for "trouble spots".

Abdominal Breathing

It's easy to forget that muscles control our breathing too. General body tension causes us to breathe in a shallow way that also causes our heart rate and jittery feelings to increase. Proper deep breathing will slow our heart rate, increase calmness and ability to concentrate.

To breathe from your abdomen:

- Find your rib cage and place one hand directly below it.
- Inhale slowly and deeply through your nose for a count of four (1-2-3-4-).
- If you are doing it properly, your abdomen will expand, your hand will rise, but your chest will be fairly still.
- Pause for a count of four trying to keep your face relaxed.
- Exhale slowly and fully through your mouth taking a count of four.
- During this practice, you might want to make a "whooo" sound.
- As you exhale, try to let your tensions go out with your breath.
- Do not gulp air but keep your breathing as smooth as possible.
- If you begin to feel dizzy, simply breathe regularly for a few minutes.

Practice this breathing technique so that you will be able to achieve it without anyone noticing. A few of these breaths just before your speech will slow your body systems and give you a sense of control.

Physical Exercise

Studies have shown that people who exercise regularly experience generally lower levels of anxiety than people who don't. Many activities such as athletic competition involve a "warm-up" period.

Adapted from: Chattanooga State's Anxiety Helpsite (http://de.cstcc.cc.tn.us/anxiety/)

Purposeful physical activity decreases the excess energy that ends to "creep out" during delivery. If we don't release the energy in positive ways it will come out in ways like fidgeting, excessive shifting of weight, and general agitation. Many professional speakers use physical activity to release stress right before a speech.

One such activity, which also uses abdominal breathing is called "The Windmill".

- Stand up straight with shoulders back and neck erect.
- Hold your arms out in front of you.
- Inhale deeply and hold your breath.
- Swing your arms backward in a circle two times.
- Swing your arms forward in a circle two times.
- Stop and exhale fully until all your air is released.
- Shrug your shoulders and release any leftover tension.

TIPS FOR MANAGING ANXIETY

1. Realize that you will not be perfectly calm. Expect a certain level of anxiety, but realize that you can manage anxiety to work to your advantage.
2. Try not to spend too much time before your presentation worrying. Don't change your regular routine.
3. Arrive at the place where you are giving your speech early enough to get organized and feel comfortable with your surroundings.
4. Talk about topics that you are interested in.
5. Be prepared. Be organized. Make sure you rehearse out loud.
6. Use highlighters to emphasize the transitions and sources on your notes.
7. Deliver your speech with the same notes with which you rehearsed. Do not rewrite the notes unless you have plenty of time to practice with the new version.
8. Use a tape recorder to practice your speech. This will allow for the development of a conversational/natural speaking style.
9. Practice standing up as though you were actually giving the speech. If possible, go to the room you will speak in and rehearse there.
10. Practice your speech out loud. The ears have sense memory just as your body does, and you will retain more of the speech if you practice aloud.
11. Avoid writing your speech out word for word. Instead, work with concepts and ideas. It is natural and desirable for a speech to be phrased somewhat differently every time it is delivered.
12. Remember to breathe and swallow during your speech. Use the "punctuation" as places to breath and/or swallow.

Adapted from: William & Mary University Oral Communication Program Website and University of Missouri Department of Communication Website.

13. If you suffer from cotton mouth, get a drink before speaking or have a throat lozenge before speaking. (Choose one that won't turn your tongue a funny color).
14. It is perfectly acceptable to pause during a speech to collect your thoughts.
15. On the day of your speech, wear clothing that is comfortable. Rehearse in the clothes you plan to wear when you deliver your speech.
16. Try to just act naturally. Be yourself and let your personality come through.
17. If there is a chance that you will play with your watch, earrings, rings, necklace, glasses, etc., take them off before giving the speech, However, don't call attention to this by waiting until your name is called for speaking.
18. Use gestures to release some of the physical tension. Don't try to freeze yourself. Practice in front of a mirror and watch your gestures.
19. If your stumble over a word or forget how to pronounce a word, simply say the word and go on with the speech. Don't call attention to it by apologizing profusely.
20. Be very familiar with your preview and transitions. If you blank in the middle of a main point, summarize it and go on to the next transition. Don't say thing like "I don't know what the next point is" or "I forgot that point." If you don't tell us, we probably won't know you forgot something.
21. Interact with your audience. Don't just speak "at" your audience, communicate with them. Eye contact is the most effective way to humanize your audience (rather than seeing them as a blurry mass of faces) and will help you to reduce your nervousness.
22. Visualize success. Imaging yourself giving the speech, and it being wildly successful. The positive associations that you develop here will continue into the actual speaking situation, and can give you a better attitude when you speak.

VISUALIZATION EXERCISE

The purpose of visualization is to refocus your mind on positive thoughts and to be more relaxed. Performers around the world including Olympic athletes, actors, and musicians use visualization. Visualization works best when you include deep breathing, and involve all of your senses in the exercise. Before we begin, think of a place that you have been before which was very relaxing. This should be a place where you felt confident and competent. Some people use the beach, some people use a forest, and some people use a house that they have been in. It is also OKAY to use a performance that you have given in the past, as long as you felt calm, confident, and competent during the performance. Let's begin.

Relaxation

Begin your deep breathing. As you breathe in, send warm rays of relaxation to the various parts of your body beginning with your feet and moving upwards. When your entire body feels relaxed then move to the next step in the exercise

Safe Place

View in your mind the place that makes you feel calm, confident, and competent. Imagine what it looks like with all the colors, shadows, etc. now imagine what you hear in the foreground and the background. Now imagine what you smell. Now imagine what you feel through the nerve endings in your body. Is there anything to taste? If so, imagine what it tastes like. Paint the picture in your mind using all of your senses. Remember to think about the fact that you have always felt calm, confident, and competent in this place.

Transition

When you feel calm, confident, and competent, begin to visualize yourself doing the speech. Imagine what you are dressed like and what the room looks like. Imagine what you have prepared perfectly and that you have begun your speech with a great deal of poise. Imagine that you know your subject matter perfectly. Imagine the audience responding to you in a positive way with smiles and nods. Imagine the sound of your voice, strong, and confident. Imagine the calmness of your body, the rhythm of your breathing, and the comfortable temperature of the room. If negative or anxiety producing thoughts enter into the visualization, move back to the relaxation step and then continue.

Choosing a Speech Topic

Remember: It's never too early to start thinking about your topic. Start NOW! You'll be grateful later.

WASHED OUT AND OVERDONE TOPICS

Some topics have been overused and overdone, or are considered trivial. Remember, in an Informative Presentation, your goal is to give your audience NEW information. If you choose a topic that has been covered extensively in newscasts, newspapers, magazines, etc., you can bet that your audience knows all that you are going to say. You need to find topics that are "out of the box." That doesn't mean your topic has to be strange or obscure. You can choose topics that relate to ECU or North Carolina, or you can choose something that has made headlines, BUT you have to dig deeper and choose an angle that sheds new light on your information. Trivial topics are those that contribute nothing to the knowledge of your audience. How to make brownies is too trivial because most people know how to make a boxed mix for brownies or cake. You would simply be telling us something we already know and have for quite some time. Also, there is not enough information about those topics to fill your time limit. In short, there's no "meat" to the topic; therefore, it's too trivial. Persuasive presentations influence the way we think, feel or behave. Choosing a topic like why we shouldn't smoke won't work because your audience has heard all of this information before. They will stop listening. Again, choose a new angle—tobacco quotas, or tobacco farming subsidies and why they should be increased or decreased or why all restaurants should be smoke free or why no restaurants should be smoke free . . .

Here is a list of topics that have been overused, overdone or are considered to be trivial. PLEASE choose something else. Your grade will thank you.

1. Sexually transmitted diseases. (These speeches turn out to be a lecture from HEALTH 101. No bananas or cucumbers and condom demonstrations are appropriate for a business presentation.)
2. Basic CPR or first aid. (We learned this in health and PE classes. Either we already know this information, or we need to learn it with a certified instructor in more than 3-5 minutes.)
3. Why being a student athlete is so hard. (No doubt there are many demands placed on student athletes, but if you are a student athlete, you chose to be one and knew the demands in advance. A student who has a full time job and who is taking 16 hours this semester would argue that they have an equally demanding lifestyle.)
4. Why fraternities and sororities are great. (No one doubts that Greek organizations play a worthwhile role in college life, and most people are aware that some Greek organizations offer more than just a place to socialize.)

5. Condom use. (What new information can you possibly add here that your audience doesn't already know?)
6. Drinking and driving. (A serious issue, of course, but your audience knows that they shouldn't drink and drive and why they shouldn't drink and drive and the penalties they face if they get caught.
7. Smoking is bad for your health. (Another serious issue but perhaps no one in your audience smokes. The topic is wasted, then. Or maybe over half of your audience smokes. They know the reasons they shouldn't. They've heard it all before.)
8. How to use the internet. (Been there and done that. We KNOW!)
9. Cell phones are a must. (Again, been there and done that. Your audience all knows what a cell phone is. Most will have one. If they don't it's because they can't afford one or simply don't want one. Cell phone etiquette is the same. People know they should not talk on their cell phone in restaurants or at the movies. Some will do it anyway.)
10. The basic rules of any sport, card game or board game. (We cannot play the sport, card game or board game with you, so the rules will be hard to understand. Also, most of your audience will already know the BASIC rules of any sport, card game or board game.)
11. Why my religion is better than yours. (Religion is a private issue for many people. What they believe is sacred to them. It is offensive for you to try to persuade someone that what they believe is not good enough or right.)
12. Seatbelt use. (We should all use our seatbelts, We know this. It's against the law NOT to buckle up. We can get hurt in an accident if we are not wearing our seat belt. We know this!)
13. Eating healthy. (We've been told to eat healthy by our parents and our health teachers. We know this.)
14. Exercise is Important. (We know this. We know that exercise reduces stress, and is good for out mental and physical health. We know that the Student Recreation Center is right on campus. Some people will still choose to be couch potatoes, and some people have a physical handicap that prevents exercise.)
15. Binge drinking. (Yes, it goes on at campus. Your audience knows what it is and what the consequences are.)
16. Organ donation/Blood donation. (Old information. It's been done and done and done . . .)
17. Using sunscreen. (We know we should. We may choose not to.)
18. Abortion/capital punishment. (These are issues that have been ruled upon by the Supreme Court. What new information can you possibly add?)
19. Drink more water. (Been there, done that. Old information.)
20. Got to college. (We're already here?!?)

THE TOPIC

The hardest part of preparing a speech is choosing a topic. For SOME assignments, your instructor might assign your topic or topic area. But for other assignments, your instructor will leave the topic choice up to you. Most students find it difficult to think of anything that they want to speak about or anything that they think their audience will want to hear. Mostly, students don't spend enough time searching for a topic. They choose whatever they just heard about or whatever is a "hot" topic at the time. These are not always the best, or the most appropriate topics to use.

Try to get "out of the box" with your topic. Don't just ask your friends what topic they'd like to hear. Listen to the news in the morning or at night, read the paper or a "newsy" magazine, listen to the news on the radio, be aware of world or political events that are affecting you as a college student.

Try brainstorming: take out a sheet of paper and write down your hobbies, favorite vacation spots, reasons that you choose your major, why you are enjoying your internship or job, what current or world events made you stop and listen to the news, etc., etc., etc. Next, narrow this list down to those topics that meet the following criteria:

1. Those things that you are truly interested in
2. Those things that you have some knowledge about
3. Those things that you can make important to your audience

Here's a BIG hint about topics—think novelty. Any audience loves to learn something new. So, choose a topic that has novelty or newness. Expand your boundaries—don't choose the same topic that your roommate chose last semester. The whole idea behind speechmaking is to communicate with your audience. Choose a topic that you can make relevant to your audience. They will thank you by listening to your speech and remembering the information.

Audience Analysis

Remember: you can't meet the needs of your audience if you don't know what they are!

WHAT IS AUDIENCE ANALYSIS AND WHY IS IT IMPORTANT?

Audience analysis is essential to great speechmaking. As a speaker, it's your job to find out as much as you can about your audience BEFORE you prepare your speech. You need this information so that you can research your topic, organize your thoughts, choose supporting material, and use the appropriate language.

Some questions that you can ask include:

1. What are the ages of the people in my audience?
2. How many men and how many women are in my audience?
3. What is the educational level of the members of my audience?
4. What are the political affiliations of my audience members?
5. What religious views do the members of my audience have?
6. Where are my audience members from?
7. What does my audience already know about my topic?
8. What does my audience need to know about this topic?
9. How can I make my speech relevant to this audience?

Once you've done your audience analysis, you'll be ready to start putting your speech together. Remember, public speaking is all about tailoring your message to your audience. When you make the information relevant to your audience, they will listen to your every word!

Speaker Credibility

"If an audience is going to believe your message, first, they have to believe in you."

TIPS FOR SPEAKER CREDIBILITY

- Consider your classroom behavior.
- Dress appropriately for the occasion.
- Incorporate your special expertise or experience.
- Use evidence to support your claims.
- Engage your audience nonverbally.
- Use powerful language.
- Use inclusive language.

ELEMENTS IN THE ARISTOTELIAN MODEL

- **Ethos:** the speaker's competence and character (source credibility)

- **Logos:** the proof a speaker offers through the words of the message

    Syllogism   Enthymeme

- **Pathos**: emotional states in an audience aroused by the speaker

    anger   fear
    kindness shame
    pity   envy

S. Brydon, M. Scott, "Elements in the Aristotelian Model". Copyright © 2000 by Mayfield Publishing Company. Reproduced with permission of The McGraw-Hill Companies.

INFORMATIVE SPEAKING

The goal of an informative speech is to add to the knowledge of your audience. There is no reason to tell them things they already know. Even if your topic is somewhat familiar to them, you should find a new twist or a new angle. If you're unsure of how much knowledge your audience has about your topic, get to class early and ask around. If you've chosen the topic of "Three benefits of eating organically grown food" and you find that 28 out of 29 students in your class already eat organically grown food, then it's time to choose something else.

Your Informative Speech is 3-6 minutes in length. In this speech, concentrate on connecting with your audience. How does your information relate to them? How will your information impact them? Why should they listen? What's in it for them? Use language that "speaks" to your audience.

*We've enclosed guidelines for your Information Speech.
Read this carefully and then use the information.
It will help!*

GUIDELINES FOR INFORMATIVE SPEECHES

- The time limit is three to six minutes.
- Three sources (individual instructor may require a different number) are required (only one website is allowed). Sources must be credible.
- Full sentence, typed outline complete with works cited page must be turned in on speech day.
- One visual aid required.
- Professional attire is required.
- The presentation must be clearly and correctly organized with an Introduction, Body and Conclusion. The Body must use one of the patterns of organization detailed in your textbook: chronological, topical, spatial, comparison—contrast, cause—effect, or problem—solution.
- Sources must be incorporated in your speech.
- Visual aids must be large enough to be seen, clean and professional looking, appropriate, useful and impactful.

POINTERS FOR YOUR INFORMATIVE SPEECH

These are the basic requirements for this assignment:

1. The Introduction should:
   a. Open with impact
   b. Orient us as to your topic
   c. Establish motivational appeal and rapport (why you are qualified and why we should listen)
   d. Preview statement

   About the Open With Impact: Always using a rhetorical question or a question that requires a show of hands can get old. **Try another strategy ... In addition, do not tell us that "Today I plan to inform you about ... " As the ad goes, "Just do it."**
2. Speech length is 3–6 minutes. FYI, speeches under or over this limit will be penalized. No exceptions. Consult your syllabus for info.
3. **Three secondary sources** (may be modified by individual instructor) are required in this speech. **Only one website** (if it is available only as an Internet source) is eligible for bibliographic citation. **One visual aid is required.**
4. A **full sentence outline** is required for this speech, as for all speeches. You must turn this in the day of your presentation and, yes, **it must be typed**. See your original syllabus if you have questions about this requirement. A major component of all outlines and for all presentations is **including your secondary sources in your outline—introducing them correctly and showing your skill in handling them.** They need to be seen and heard. Obviously, you will need to reference all three sources, that is, cite them during your presentation.
5. Include your Works Cited as a separate attachment to your **outline—titled "Works Cited."**
6. Include copies of your secondary sources with your outlines, attached to your bibliography (If your instructor requires them).
7. Yes, you need a preview statement. Yes, it occupies the place of honor . . . last sentence in your introductory paragraph.
8. Everyone can benefit from working on **transition words, phrases, and sentences.** Transitions move us (and you) from main point to main point. They also connect ideas in a speech.
9. Ethically Compelling and Emotionally Compelling **are two additional areas that we all can work on. You need to state (not ask us to infer or imply) the reasons (as you develop and support each of your major points) that your audience should care about your position . . . Make it relevant to the . . . connect it to them . . . More than once.**
10. **Professional dress is required.**

PUBLIC SPEAKING DO'S AND DON'TS FOR EXECUTIVES

Know Your Audience, Anticipate Questions and Rehearse

Lisa Lee Freeman

You may not be aware of it, but the next time you give a speech, odds are minds will wander and eyes will glaze over. Snores may even rip through the crowd.

And it's probably your own fault, say experts in public speaking.

Audiences do tend to have exceedingly short attention spans nowadays—what with channel—surfing having become a national pastime. But the real problem is likely to be your presentation skills.

"Ninety percent of speeches are boring," said New York executive speech coach Ralph Proodian.

Be boring if you want. But be prepared to suffer the consequences, which can include angering your audience, failing to get your point across and appearing incompetent, warn speech consultants.

For those interested in keeping audiences on their toes—or at least in their seats—the following are some suggestions:

- **Get to the point quickly.** "Respect your audience's time," said Jon Kranshar of Alies Communications, a speech consulting firm in New York. People have short attention spans; so "opt for less time, not more. End early and your audiences will be grateful."

- **Analyze your audience in advance.** When preparing a presentation, Kranshar says, ask yourself such questions as: What information do they need? And what do I want to happen as a result of the talk.

- **Never jump right into a presentation.** Step up to the lectern and give the audience a few seconds to look you over, while you glance around the room and check them out. "It's called taking the platform and it's very powerful," said Dorothea Johnson, director of The Protocol School of Washington.

- **Don't open with,** "Good morning, it's a pleasure to be here in Peoria," instead, try something provocative. "In the past, they used to say start with a joke," said Terry Van Tell, a New York executive communications consultant. But you shouldn't use humor unless you can pull it off. Another idea: Start with a question and ask listeners to respond by raising their hands.

© 2005 Investor's Business Daily, Inc. You may not copy, modify, redistribute, or display these materials without the written consent of Investor's Business Daily. Investor's Business Daily and its licensors expressly disclaim any express or implied warranties or representations regarding the accuracy, completeness, timeliness, or reliability of information, facts, views, opinions or recommendations contained in this publication.

- **Use appropriate hand gestures.** "When you make a gesture it should mean something," said Johnson. Vertical hand chops can be used for emphasis. But never point at the audience; it's a put-down. "President Clinton would point until an advisor taught him to close his hand and use his thumb instead," noted Johnson. "Also, any gesture below the waist is negative."
- **Use effective eye contact.** "You want to have your eyes on the audience 90% of the time," says New York presentation coach Dorothy Sarnoff. "You should be pivoting your head so your eyes sweep across the audience. It's like an embrace to the listeners." But don't focus too long on anyone. Also, don't let your eyes flit across the room like a typewriter carriage.
- **Don't lean.** Johnson recalled looking on in astonishment as an ambassador "leaned across and wrapped his entire arms around the lectern." Leaning on anything while you speak destroys your power and authority, she says.
- **Keep your hands free.** Lose the pens and pointers, advises Johnson. "Any time you have an object in your hand it detracts from what you're saying."
- **Never take a drink while facing your audience.** It's distracting. Also, peering over the rim of a cup makes you look unsophisticated. If you must wet your whistle, turn to the side before taking a sip.
- **Pay close attention to your feet.** "The way you stand says a lot about you," said Johnson. Proper foot placement helps a speaker keep his or her balance and poise, she says. Try standing with your feet at least one foot apart and your right foot about two to three inches in front of your left foot. A good way to project a solid image and keep yourself from rocking back and forth on your feet is to "Imagine your feet are in cement," said Brian Carlsen, an education manager at Arthur Anderson in St. Charles, Ill.
- **Keep shoulders straight in front of an audience.** Holding them at an angle makes you look ambivalent, says, Carlsen, who runs a course called "Effective Presentations."
- **Use props.** Van Tell says one client used a sheet of paper to illustrate her firm's shrinking market share. "She ripped it in half and said, `This was our market share in 1992.' She ripped it again and said, `This was our market share in 1993.' Finally, with just a scrap left, she said, 'This is our market share today.'"
- **Heed the "Theory of Three."** "Studies have been done about what people can tolerate," said Van Tell. "They can tolerate three but feel cheated by two and overwhelmed by four." So try to break your speech down to three main points.
- **Anticipate questions, especially tough ones.** "Handling Q&A is an art form," said Van Tell. "If you get a hostile question, always paraphrase it for the audience and take out the hostility." And if you can't answer it, say it's too complex to cover right now, or tell them you'll look into it and get back to

them at a later date or after the presentation. Then break eye contact. "Don't go back and say, 'Did I answer your question?' And remember to keep a pleasant tone of voice."

- **Never pause in the middle of a sentence.** "You don't want to say, for example, John . . . went home," said speech coach, Ralph Proodian. Speakers often stop at the wrong places when they're reading word-for-word off a cue card. It makes you sound like you really don't know what you're taking about and it takes the expression out of your voice.
- **Don't deliberately deepen your voice.** It strains the vocal chords and causes you to speak in an uninflected monotone voice. "And you come across belligerent," said Proodian. Also, poor inflection, or a failure to emphasize key words, weakens your message, he complains "The voice is the key to meaning." Noted Johnson, "What you say communicates only 7% of your message to an audience. How you say it or your tone of voice communicates 38%. The remaining 55% is body language."
- **Keep the microphone below your chin.** "The more of you the audience can see, the stronger your image," says Proodian.
- **Rehearse, rehearse and rehearse some more.** And make sure the last time you rehearse is as close to the delivery time as possible, so that it's in your system," stressed Sarnoff.

EXAMPLE OF AN INFORMATIVE SPEECH ASSIGNMENT

Objective

Your goal in this assignment is to present information about a career field or service that you are interested in. This information should be presented in a way so the members of the audience will be interested, will understand the information, and will remember your message. You may choose career field you are interested in and are pursuing after college or a different one. Please remember that this speech does require outside research so make sure you choose a field that you will have access to pretty readily.

Due Date: _____

Informative Speeches

Remember that information means *new*. The type of career may be familiar to the audience, such as Nursing or Teaching. The audience may not be familiar with the impact this career has on lives, or the day in and day outs of the life of someone in this career. The audience will be interested in personal information about your chosen career or field, what issues are facing your career field today and specific information or case study about a particular company or place of business that is in your field. Your challenge is to provide new twists, new perspectives, or a deeper understanding of your career path. Give them something to think about.

Remember that audiences will listen better to information they believe is ***relevant***. As you gather information regarding this career or field, ask yourself how the audience members are affected by the career or new information about this job area. Relate the benefits of this field to the needs and interests of your audience members. *Note that stories and vivid descriptions hold attention. You can bring your information to life by employing these methods!

Guidelines

Time: 3–6 minutes

Sources: Minimum of three sources

Outline: Typed, double-spaced, full sentence, correct format (see handout provided), complete bibliography in APA format

Notecards: For speech presentation

Visual Aid: Not required

PERSUASIVE SPEAKING

The goal of persuasive speaking is to limit the options your audience perceives as acceptable. You want your audience to WANT to choose the position you are advocating.

So, just like in Informative Speaking, connect with your audience. Motivate them to listen—show them how your topic will affect them. Tell them "what's in it for them."

Use strong persuasive language. Words like "should," "need to," "must," and "ought to" are the norm in persuasion.

Draw a picture in the minds of your audience members and involve them emotionally.

GUIDELINES FOR PERSUASIVE SPEECHES

- Time is 5–7 minutes, Your goal is to influence your audience (the way they think, act or behave).
- Two visual aids required.
- Six sources required (individual instructor may require a different number), only one website allowed. All six sources must be incorporated in your speech.
- Counterarguments are required—at least one, but ideally, one for each main point.
- Emotional and logical appeals to your listeners are required.
- Typed, full sentence outline with works cited page attached is required.
- Organization must be correct, including an Introduction, Body and Conclusion. The body of your speech must follow a clear pattern of organization as detailed in your text: topical, cause–effect, problem–solution.

POINTERS FOR YOUR PERSUASIVE SPEECH

Keep the following pointers and suggestions in mind as you prepare and practice your persuasive presentations.

Length of presentation is 5–7 minutes, with a 30 second window on the post seven-minute side if instructor allows. Secondary sources to be cited orally during presentation and be identifiable as such in your outline. two relevant, well managed, and timely visual aids are required.

Persuasion is an attempt to limit the options that are perceived as acceptable. It is not an attempt to simply inform or to coerce; coercion excludes options, while informing increases the number of choices or options.

Persuasive presentations are most successful when they are based on a speaker's understanding of the relationship between ethos, logos, and pathos and how these elements connect to an audience. As always, start with your audience . . . what are your goals (i.e. what is the rhetorical situation)?

Ethos is primarily the responsibility of the speaker . . . establishing your competency and character, which confirms for your audience that you are credible and trustworthy. The kinds of evidence that you cite, your attire, your conduct, (everything from being an attentive listener to arriving on time for class shape this audience's perceptions of credible conduct), your language (and your vocal variety), your nonverbal behaviors (especially eye contact and posture) contribute to building and confirming competency and character.

Logos, the words and therefore the logic of your persuasive appeal are also the primary responsibility of the speaker. Again the kind of evidence that you present is crucial to your appeal's success. As well, you must make every effort to convey that your topic is relevant to your audience and that it is presented in an ethical manner which can be understood and comprehended by your audience. Review our discussion about the kinds of evidence that audiences find most persuasive. Adapt this knowledge to your presentation. Remember to take steps that encourage elaborated thinking on the part of your audience. You are most likely to be persuasive if you use a two-sided appeal.

Pathos, the emotion(s) that you produce in your audience, should help you achieve your persuasive goal. By the way, this is an opportunity to remind you that YOU must know what you want your audience to do, think, believe or feel. Are you reinforcing a belief they already hold? Are you attempting to inoculate? Do you want them to act? Do you want to change an attitude? Without this awareness and without clearly conveying this goal to your audience in your preview statement, your persuasive appeal is destined for failure. Back to pathos . . . what emotional appeal(s) do you wish to make? To pride? To shame? To calmness? To loyalty? To fear? To kindness? The possibilities are as long as the list of emotions. Be cautious about evoking excessive fear . . . remember what studies suggest about fear overload. Are there primitive and conditioned responses that you can ethically elicit from your audience?

Finally, be aware that your goal must be achievable for your audience. So as you know . . . analyze the diversity of your audience, their level of involvement with your topic and their willingness to be motivated by your appeal.

EXAMPLE OF A PERSUASIVE SPEECH ASSIGNMENT

This speech is designed to persuade the audience of a proposition, fact, value or policy. This assignment requires considerable research and skillful handling of methods of persuasion. Choose an issue of significance, an issue or problem in which you believe. You will be using one of the following organizational patterns in order to reach your persuasive goal: Monroe's Motivated Sequence, problem solution, cause–effect, or three reasons. Please pick a topic that you feel is important but that can also move/persuade your audience in the time limit provided. This speech gives you an opportunity to affect the attitudes and/or behaviors of your audience. Remember your topic must be something that your audience will view as relative! ! ! ! !

Due Date _____

Guidelines

- 5–7 minutes
- Sources: minimum of six sources (two of which can be Internet) You must have a variety of **types** of sources
- Visual aid
- Typed, double spaced, and in complete sentences outline
- Complete works cited page in APA format

Evaluation Criteria

- Must be persuasive in your reasons
- Variety of research
- Cite sources correctly in outline and oral speech
- Reasons support persuasive appeal
- **Must connect with audience**
- Use emotional appeal
- Transitions are clear
- Thesis is stated clearly
- Persuasive organizational pattern is clear
- Counter arguments are required
- Introduction and conclusion are strong
- Appropriate topic for audience and time limit

Speech Outlines

Full sentence outlines are mandatory for the two speeches you will do. These must be typed and they must include a works cited page.

This handbook contains two examples of full sentence outlines. These outlines may be covered in class by your instructor, but you need to read over them and familiarize yourself with the format we use. Use them as a guide for your own outlines, and you should be in good shape.

Good outlines are essential to a well-organized speech.

PERSUASIVE SALES SPEECH

Topic: Gillette razors

General Purpose: To sell

Specific Purpose: To sell my audience Gillette razors because they leave your skin feeling smooth, have new technology, and are inexpensive for all that they come with. Central Idea: Gillette razors leave your skin feeling smooth, have new technology, and are inexpensive for the package they come in.

INTRODUCTION

I. Attention grabber—Do you want to look like this? (gorilla picture)
II. Topic—If you're like me and you don't, than you should buy a Gillette razor.
III. Credibility and Good will—I have used the Venus Gillette razor for over three years now and recommend that and the Mach3 Turbo for males to each of you for the closest shave you've ever had.
IV. Preview—You must buy a Venus or Mach3 Turbo razor because they will leave your skin feeling smooth, they come with new technology, and they are inexpensive considering all that they come with.

BODY

I. The first reason you should each buy a Gillette razor is because they will leave your skin feeling smoother than ever before.
   A. You don't have to worry about getting cuts after using these razors.
      1. Counterargument—You may think that any razor can give you a cut, despite the safety precautions used.
      2. Paul Sheetz, an owner of Mach3 Turbo, states: "Before buying Mach3 Turbo, I was the king of putting toilet paper over the cuts on my face to stop the bleeding. Now, it doesn't even take effort to avoid cutting myself."

B. You can also use Gillette razors to shave in the more sensitive areas of the body.

   1. Emotional appeal—Ladies, imagine that you bought the most fantastic bating suit you could find for your trip to Greece this summer. You're around an attractive guy when you reveal the bathing suit, and all you can see is razor burn everywhere!
   2. The Venus razor for women is designed especially to twist and turn with the curves of the body in order to avoid that irritating and embarrassing rash.

Transition; Now that you understand why these razors can benefit you, let's examine how they are designed differently from other razors.

II. The second reason you must buy the Venus or Mach3 Turbo is that they come with a special technology that no other razor had before them.

   A. The design of the Gillette razors are for the user's safety and easy-to-use.

      1. According to Gillette, the head of the razor includes a skin-softening lubricated strip, three close shaving blades, and soft cushions for a closer shave.
      2. The razor is easy to use because of a gripped handle, pivoting razor head, and button for simple replacement of blades.

   B. Counterargument—You're probably looking up at me thinking why in the world would you need a razor that comes with all of these advancements.

      1. Emotional Appeal—Ladies, why buy makeup if you don't want your face to look the best? Gentlemen, why buy cologne of you don't want to smell your best. I ask you then, why buy a razor if it doesn't make your skin look the best?
      2. The people of Gillette work day and night to think of new ideas that will help their consumers get the best out of their products.

Transition: Since we have now covered what the Gillette razors can do for you and what they are made of, let's discuss the prices of these items.

III. Finally, you should each go out and buy a Gillette razor because the cost of the Venus and Mach3 Turbo is cheap when you look at all that they come with.

   A. According to the Eckerd on 14th and Charles in Greenville, North Carolina, both the Venus razor and the Mach 3 cost $8.

      1. The razors come with a shower storage system as well as extra blades.
      2. According to the USA Today article, "Gillette Hopes To Power Shaver Sales to Women With Vibrance," the Venus and Mach3 Turbo made a combined. 21 million dollars in 2004. This would not be the case if their consumers didn't continue to buy from them.

B. Counterargument—In some of your heads you might be wondering how a razor could cost $8.

1. Emotional Appeal—I understand that we are all college students and that money is not growing from trees for us. This purchase, however, is worth its price and will leave you feeling satisfied.
2. Kathleen, an ECU student that uses the Venus razor explains; "The $8 that I could spend on other purchases, I decide to spend on making my skin feel the best that it can without hurting myself. It may not be worth it to some people, but it gives me more confidence to know that I had a smooth shave, especially with summer coming up."

CONCLUSION

I. In overview, you should each purchase a Gillette razor because they leave your skin feeling smooth, come with the best technology, and are moderately priced for the package they come in.
II. Don't look like him (hold up gorilla), go out and buy a Gillette razor today!

SAMPLE OUTLINE FOR A PERSUASIVE SPEECH USING MONROE'S MOTIVATED SEQUENCE METHOD

INTRODUCTION

I. Attention: Have you ever slept through a meeting? Have you ever felt too tired to go out with friends? Have you ever fallen asleep trying to study, or even during class? Are you sleeping now?
II. Topic: With all of the events and activities that fill our schedules each day, there is a huge need for us to prioritize sleep.
III. Relevance of topic: I'm sure that when you sit down with your schedules which are jam packed with study, work, and hanging out, the first thing to get cut back is sleep.
IV. Credibility: As a full time college student with a job, I have often cut back on sleep to get other things done. However, I have also run into the problem of being tired the next day. Unfortunately, being tired is not the only problem associated with sleep-loss.
V. Preview statement: Sleep deprivation can cause many health and social problems; therefore, the solution would be to prioritize sleep in daily life and with that would come many benefits.

BODY

I. Need: Many college students do not get near enough sleep, which is detrimental to your health and social life.

   A. Many students do not get near enough sleep, this much is obvious by attendance in classes, the alarm clocks that never go off in the dorms, and the number of students who stay up late throughout the week to go downtown.

      1. Other obvious signs that they are being sleep deprived are the blank stares, falling asleep in class, and snapping at friends.

   B. Ramification: Without sleep your body ceases to function normally and weakens your immune system, in addition to that lack of sleep makes you irritable and drowsy.

      1. The Medical Editorial Board states that sleep deprivation "can interfere with memory, energy levels, mental abilities, and emotional mood."
      2. A study conducted by the University of Chicago Medical Center indicates that the "condition drastically affects the body's ability to metabolize glucose, leading to symptoms that mimic early-stage diabetes."

   C. Pointing: This problem is rampant among high school and college age students in particular, but is also increasing in other areas too.

      1. According to a CCN health article, "America's sleep problems have reached epidemic proportions, and may be the country's number-one health problem."
      2. Clearly this is something that we need to be concerned about now, because too many people rank sleep too low on their priority list.

Transition: Severe sleep loss is an issue that concerns us all and that few take seriously; however, there is a very simple solution to this problem.

II. Satisfaction: The solution to this problem would be for people to prioritize sleep in their daily lives.

   A. We should make it a priority to get the recommended amount of sleep each night.

      1. According to a WebMD article "experts say that 7 to 9 hours is the recommended amount of sleep."
      2. This may seem like a lot of time, but in order to be fully functioning, and feel rested the next day, it is a necessity.

B. Making sure that sleep is a priority by getting the recommended amount of sleep each night is easy and effective.

1. All one needs to do it go to bed at a regular hour each night.
2. Don't sleep throughout the day, but only at night, so that your body will become conditioned to being restful.

C. Some of you may argue that getting that much sleep is impossible with the amount of work and activities that you plan each day and night.

1. However, if you took out all the time that you spend taking naps, and all the extra time it takes to do things because you are to lethargic to do them efficiently, then you would realize that you probably waste as much time as you would spend sleeping.
2. If you had had a healthy night's sleep, you would be able to get your work done quicker and actually end up with more time to do what you needed to during the day.

Transition: The benefits to getting enough sleep are clear and expansive.

III. Visualization: How many of you feel groggy, as though clouds were filling up your head, now picture those clouds floating away, leaving your mind clear and your body limber and quick.

A. Positive: You don't have to imagine this effect; it can be a reality when you get the recommended amount of sleep.

1. The National Sleep Foundation reports that "Sufficient sleep helps us think more clearly, complete complex tasks better and more consistently and enjoy everyday life more fully."

B. Negative: Not getting enough sleep, on the other hand has hugely detrimental effects.

1. Sleepiness has negative effects that begin with simple embarrassment when your face hits the desk, or you wake up in a pool of your own drool.
2. But they can get much more serious, for example, the National Sleep Foundation also states that a lack of sleep is "associated with reduced short-term memory and learning ability, negative mood, inconsistent performance, poor productivity and loss of some forms of behavioral control"

C. Comparison of positive and negative: The choice between being healthy and mentally stable and being sick and irritable is as simple as going to bed.

1. Sara Ross, graduate student at ECU finds the choice even simpler, she says, "sleep or die."

CONCLUSION

I. Action: In conclusion I urge you to take that action, and make that choice.

    A. Summarize main points: Sleep deprivation is associated with many health risks, as well as social problems.

    B. Statement of desired action or attitude change: Therefore the need to prioritize sleep in our lives is an obvious solution to this issue.

    C. lose with impact: Ultimately, as stated in the Better Sleep Guidebook sleep "affects all aspects of your day—from how you feel, to your relationships, productivity, and ultimately, your quality of life." So tonight, sleep well.

WORKS CITED

1. http://www.sleep-deprivation.com/
2. CNN Health Watch Article. Lack of Sleep is America's Top Health Problem. http://www.cnn.com/HEALTH/9703/17/nfm/sleep.deprivation/index.html
3. WebMD article on sleep. http://my.webmd.com/content/Article/102/106908.htm
4. http://www.sleepfoundation.org/_content/hottopics/sleep_and_teens_reportl.pdf
5. http://www.bettersleep.org/pdfs/2004-better-sleep-guide.pdf
6. Sara Jane Ross: graduate student

SAMPLE OUTLINE FORMAT:
MONROE'S MOTIVATED SEQUENCE

INTRODUCTION

I. Attention—really work to make the audience sit up and listen to your speech.
II. Topic—what are you going to persuade us to do or think?
III. Relevance of topic—show your audience how or why this affects them.
IV. Credibility—why are you qualified to give this speech?
V. Preview statement—preview your main points exactly as you will discuss them

BODY

I. Need (describes problem in a way that motivates the audience to see a need for change)

   A. Statement of problem—details, description

      1. stories, examples, statistics
      2. same
      3. same if necessary

   B. Ramification—what are the consequences of this problem?

      1. supporting material
      2. same
      3. same if necessary

   C. Pointing—make it clear to the audience how they are directly affected by this problem and why they should care.

      1. support
      2. same
      3. same

Transition

II. Satisfaction—(presents a specific solution)

   A. Statement of proposed solution

      1. support
      2. same

B. Explanation of solution

　　1. support
　　2. same
　　3. same

C. Meeting objections (anticipate objection, address and refute them)

　　1. support
　　2. same

Transition

III. Visualization (paint a mental picture for your audience)

　A. Positive—how things will change for the better if your plan is adopted

　　1. support
　　2. same

　B. Negative what will the negative consequences be if your plan is not adopted?

　　1. support
　　2. support

　C. Comparison of the positive and the negative

　　1. examples and support
　　2. same

CONCLUSION

I. Action—provide a call to action

　A. Summarize main points
　B. Statement of desired action or attitude change
　C. Close with impact

WORKS CITED

INFORMATIVE SPEECH OUTLINE

Topic: _____

General Purpose: _____

Specific Purpose: _____

INTRODUCTION

I. **Capture attention**—ask a question, make a startling statement, use a visual aid, etc. Do NOT begin with, "Hi, my name is . . . and today I'm going to talk about . . . "
II. **Orientation**—a one sentence synopsis of what your speech is about.
III. **Connect with your audience** and state your credibility (Rapport and Motivation)—show your audience how your speech will benefit them. What will they get out of it? Then tell them why you are qualified to give this speech. Why should we believe you?
IV. **Preview your main points**—Tell your audience what you will cover in the body of your speech.

BODY

I. Statement of first main point. This is a complete sentence.

   A. Statement of first subpoint. A subpoint provides support for your main point. Remember, main points cannot stand alone. You have to back them up with statistics, quotes, facts, additional statements, etc.

      1. Statement of supporting point. A supporting point provides additional support for the main point and the subpoint.
      2. Another supporting point.
      3. Perhaps even another. This is optional.

   B. This is your second subpoint. This is a mandatory point. Remember, for every A there is a B, and for every 1. there is always a 2.

      1. supporting point
      2. supporting point
      3. supporting point

   C. You may have another subpoint here or A and B may be enough. It will depend on your information and the amount of time you have.

      1. supporting point
      2. supporting point
      3. supporting point

Transition: This is a statement that bridges main points I and I. It leads your audience from one point to another.

II. Statement of second main point. A full, complete sentence.

    A. First subpoint

        1. first supporting point
        2. supporting point
        3. supporting point

    B. Subpoint

        1. supporting point
        2. supporting point

Transition

III. Statement of third main point here.

    A. subpoint

        1. supporting point
        2. supporting point

    B. subpoint

        1. supporting point
        2. supporting point

CONCLUSION

I. Summary of main points. It's okay to say. "In conclusion, . . . " You can say, "Today we have looked at the three ways to . . . ."

II. Close with impact.

WORKS CITED

PERSUASIVE SPEECH OUTLINE

Name: _____

Topic: _____

General Purpose: _____

Specific Purpose: _____

INTRODUCTION

I. My attention gabbing statement! ! !
II. Orientation step: reveal topic
III. I state my credibility—why I am qualified AND I connect with my audience.(This is where I tell them how this speech will benefit them . . .) Rapport and Motivation
IV. One statement that clearly previews my main points.

BODY

I. Full sentence statement of first main point.

   A. Support for main point.

      1. More support—maybe a statistic, a fact or an example.
      2. More and more support.

   B. Counterargument —anticipate possible objections to your argument in the minds of your listeners. You can say, "Now, some of you may be thinking . . ." OR "Some of you may have heard the opposing argument that so and so has put out there . . ."

      1. Here's where you tell them why their objections are unfounded by continuing to build your argument.
      2. More support.

Transition: Now that we have looked at . . . let's turn to . . .

II. Full sentence statement of second main point.

   A. Support here.

      1. Counterargument for second main point.
      2. More support.

B. Support for your second point.

1. Support.
2. Support.

Transition: Now that . . . , let's . . .

III. Full sentence statement of third main point.

A. Add support

1. Support.
2. Support.

B. Additional support for main point.

1. Counterargument here.
2. Objection satisfied.

CONCLUSION

I. Summary of main points as they were previewed and developed.
II. Close with impact.

WORKS CITED

SPECIFIC PURPOSE AND CENTRAL IDEA EXERCISES

Below are two central ideas for speeches. For each central idea provide the general purpose, specific purpose, and main points of the speech.

General Purpose:

Specific Purpose:

Central Idea: The four stages of alcoholism are the warning stage, the danger stage, the crucial stage, and the chronic stage.

Main Points:

General Purpose:

Specific Purpose:

Central Idea: You should join a sorority or fraternity because of the social, academic, and economic benefits.

Main Points:

Stephan Lucas, *The Art of Public Speaking Workbook,* © The McGraw-Hill Companies.

SPEECH PREPARATION

Good speeches don't just happen. You may wish they did . . . but they don't, won't, and never will. You have to take time to prepare a speech.

Careful preparation will be reflected in the grade you receive for each speech. Speeches put together the night before your presentation will be unorganized, unprofessional and easily recognizable.

Just follow the advice we give and start at the beginning . . .

HOW DO I GET THERE FROM HERE?

If you feel overwhelmed about giving a speech, DON'T! Most people do, so you're among friends. Just take it step by step and you'll be fine.

1. Choose a topic. Refer to your book for the guidelines for selecting a topic, but first and foremost, make sure it is something that you are interested in. Then make sure you know something about your topic—a little knowledge goes a long way! Next, think appropriateness—you're going to be in a business situation most of the time when you speak, what topic would be appropriate for your audience? Finally, can you manage the topic in the time available? Narrow this topic down—choose three areas you wish to discuss—these will be your main points.
2. Research your topic. This means finding more information than just what you know. You're looking for facts, statistics, examples, opinions from other sources that agree with what you are saying, or that add to the information you already have.
3. Choose how you will organize your speech. Will you use Time Pattern? Spatial? Topical? Problem-Solution? Causal? Which main point will you talk about first? Which will come in the middle? Which will go last? All major information goes in the body—this is where you support your thesis statement.
4. Write your speech out beginning with your Introduction, then the Body, then the Conclusion. Go ahead and write it out word for word so you can see what you've got. Include all sources. Sources are when you give credit for information that is not your own. You cite these by saying, "According to . . ." or "As cited in the book . . ."
5. Look over what you've written. Does it flow? Are your main points logical? Do you support each main point with sub points and supporting points? Do you use a variety of support such as examples, statistics, facts, etc. to appeal to the greatest number of people? Do you use transitions to flow from main point to main point? Do you have a strong opening statement? How about a strong closing statement?

6. Take your manuscript speech and put it in outline form on paper. Once this is done, and you're sure your outline is correctly done, start practicing this out loud and use a stop watch or a watch with a second hand so that you can time your speech. Too long? What can you cut out? Too short? Where can you add information? Do it again and time it again . . . and again, etc.
7. Once you are satisfied with the time of your speech, convert this to your notecards. Try NOT to write it out word for word, but use phrases or words. You should practice your speech until you are so familiar with it that all you have to do is see the word or phrase and you will know what you want to say.
8. Choose a visual aid that clarifies one of your main points. Visuals can be posters, flip charts, overhead transparencies, video tapes, handouts, etc. If you use a visual, you must explain it. Do not pass things around. Visual aids go in the body of the speech.
9. Practice your speech until you hate it. Put it away, then pull it out the next day and practice again.
10. Visualize yourself doing your speech well. Remember, positive self talk is what you want. Perfection is NOT the goal. Communicating with your audience is the goal.

TOASTMASTERS INTERNATIONAL
"BE PREPARED TO SPEAK" CHECKLIST

Speechwriting

Step 1: Know Your Audience

1. How large will your audience be?
2. What are the age and educational ranges of your audience?
3. What are the chief social and financial concerns of your audience?
4. Will your listeners be predominately men or women?
5. What types of employment do your listeners have?
6. What types of hobbies or other interests do your listeners have?
7. Why does this group meet? What common interests bring the members together?
8. What other characteristics typify this audience?

Step 2: Know the Occasion

1. Is the occasion solemn, formal, or casual?
2. Is an event being celebrated?
3. Does the audience hope to be informed, entertained, or inspired? Or do they hope for some combination of the three?
4. Will a meal be served, and, if so, will you speak before or after the meal?
5. Is there a guest of honor?
6. Will there be other speakers, and, if so, in what order will you speak?
7. How important is your role? Are you the featured speaker?
8. How long of a speech does the program chairman expect?

Step 3: Know Your Speaking Environment

1. How large of a room will you be in?
2. Will the audience be sitting in rows of chairs, at tables, or will they be standing?
3. Will you be on a stage or podium, or at a head table?
4. Will you have a lectern?
5. Will you have a microphone, and, if so, will it be portable or fixed?
6. Exactly where will you be, where will the audience be, and where will the guest of honor, the person who introduces you, and other important guests be?

Step 4: Pin Down Your Topic

1. What information do you have that would provide most benefit to the group members?
2. What information do you have which you are most enthusiastic about sharing with the audience?
3. Why did the group ask *you* to speak?

4. How can you adapt your special knowledge so that it will both fulfill the expectations of the audience and appeal to their special interests?
5. Is your purpose to inform, persuade, entertain, or inspire? Or is it some combination of the above?

Step 5: Brainstorm

1. Have you included stories, examples, illustrations, and factual evidence?
2. Have you included illustrations from your personal experience?
3. Have you developed more ideas than you will actually need for your speech?

Step 6: Research

1. Have you assembled the necessary facts and statistics to make your case convincing?
2. Have you assembled quotes or testimonials from respected sources who agree with you?
3. Have you made use of the materials in your own library?
4. Have you called friends or trade organizations that might have currently updated information?
5. Have you made use of your reference librarian?
6. Have you absolutely assured yourself that all your facts and statistics are accurate and current?

Step 7: Prepare a Rough Draft of Your Speech

Introduction

1. Is your introduction dramatic, humorous, or unusual enough to grab your audience's attention?
2. Does your introduction include a single sentence that clearly states your topic?
3. Does your introduction conclude with a clear and simple statement of your point of view?
4. Is your language clear and vivid enough to assure your audience that your speech will be entertaining and well organized?

Discussion

5. Does the discussion section of your speech provide the necessary evidence for your audience to agree with your point of view?
6. Does your discussion concentrate on developing a few points clearly and precisely?
7. Have you organized your discussion section so that your main points develop in a logical sequence or so that the dramatic level builds?
8. Have you used anecdotes, stories, humorous observations, or illustrations to help your audience visualize the meaning of facts and statistics?

Conclusion

9. Have you cued your audience that your conclusion is forthcoming?
10. Have you briefly summarized the very most important points of your presentation?
11. Have you clearly and explicitly stated exactly what actions you would like your listeners to take?
12. Have you left your audience with a dramatic flourish that makes your speech memorable?

Speech Presentation

Step 8: Transfer Your Speech to Mental or Written Notes

1. Have you included one word, short phrase, symbol, or letter to remind you of each section of your speech?
2. Have you avoided the temptation to include sentences or whole segments of your speech?
3. Have you made your notes easy to read, with big lettering and plenty of open space?
4. Have you clearly numbered each card or sheet?
5. Have you written out all numbers or quotes, which need to be cited exactly?

Step 9: Practice

1. Have you created conditions as similar as possible to your actual speaking environment?
2. Have you imagined those features of the audience you cannot simulate, things like the full-sized room, faces, the lighting, and the location of the microphone?
3. Have you practiced varying your eye contact among four or five locations distributed throughout the room and holding your eye contact for several seconds at each location?
4. Have you exaggerated variations in the pitch, rate, and volume of your speaking during the practice sessions?
5. Have you exaggerated gestures and forced yourself to use them in every sentence during some of your practice sessions?
6. Have you recorded yourself on video, or audio, tape and evaluated your performance?
7. Have you practiced before an audience of at least one?
8. Have you practiced to the point where your notes are virtually unnecessary?

Control Your Nervousness

Step 10: Beyond Nervousness

1. Have you imagined your audience responding *exactly* how you want them to, eager faces, laughter, applause, standing ovation, requests for more information, requests for order forms, handing over checks, asking questions, thanking you, etc.?
2. Have you accepted the fact you may have nervous symptoms on the day of your speech, and gone on to the much more important business of sharing your knowledge and enthusiasm with your audience?
3. Have you reviewed the ten steps and assured yourself that you've done everything necessary to assure an expert speech?

TIPS FOR SPEAKING

Some tips for speaking based on the first round of speeches:

1. **PowerPoint**—The most overused, wrongly used, inefficient technology in recent years. There is a right way and a wrong way to use PowerPoint. The wrong way includes:

   ◆ Even attempting to use it on your speech day if you are not 105% positive you know how and have used it before.

   ◆ Letting someone else be responsible for changing your slide. IF you use pp, you move it close enough to the lectern so that YOU control the mouse. A speaker NEVER gives someone else the power to ruin their speech. You stay in control of all your visuals at all times.

   ◆ Putting up a slide and ignoring it. IF you put up a slide, it is for the purpose of supplementing your material or explaining your point. IF it goes up, you MUST refer to it and explain it.

2. **Visuals**—The purpose of a visual is to clarify a point, help your audience understand and remember and add interest. If your visual doesn't do these things, then it needs to stay at home. The wrong way to use visuals includes:

   ◆ Putting them where the audience can see them ahead of time. If you do this, where do you think we are looking? Your attention getter will not make an impact if we are not listening. We will NOT listen to you if there is something we can look at.

   ◆ Putting them low down on the easel where those people in the back half of the class simply can't see them. Another problem is placing objects on the table in front of the lectern. We CAN'T see these unless we are in the front row.

   ◆ Never referring to the visual. We will NOT understand it or know what we are looking at if you don't refer to your visual and explain it.

   ◆ Waiting to refer to your visual after your conclusion. Visual aids function to clarify material. To help us remember your information. IF you don't use them in your speech, you have failed to use visuals correctly. They are useless at this point.

   ◆ Using visuals that look like you made them 10 minutes before class. If they look sloppy and unprofessional, we will ignore them, think you made them at the last minute, and we won't think you are a credible speaker. Think we won't notice? Don't kid yourself!

3. **Sources**—Without sources, your speech is plagiarized. If the idea, statement or thought is not your original thought, idea or statement, then you must give credit for the idea, statement or thought. You MUST say out loud in your speech: "According to Dr. Michael Benton at Pitt County Memorial Hospital, ..." OR "As stated in the book *Love Hurts* by Petunia Dewey, ..." These same sources MUST be seen on the outline. Then they are listed on the works cited page.
4. **Delivery**—If you are bored during your speech, we will be also. If you read your paper to us, that is not a speech. With a speech, you bring the words on the paper to life. You LOOK at us and you TALK to us. You vary your rate, pitch, intensity. You increase and decrease your volume. You pause between points rather than talking as fast as you can so that you can sit down.

TIPS FOR SPEAKING . . . THE SECOND TIME!

Well, you've each completed at least one speech by now, and some of you are pleased with your grade, and some of you are not! I'd like for you to take a few minutes and review the following information before you give your Persuasive Speech. Ask yourself these questions:

1. Did I choose a topic that broke new ground? One that wasn't "Today's Headlines"? Did I shed new light on an old topic, or did I give my audience new information? Did I teach them something they didn't know? Was I interested in my topic? Did I have some knowledge about my topic? Could I get excited and enthusiastic about my topic?
2. Did I follow the sample outlines gone over in class? Or did I just use whatever program was on my computer? Did I use clear outline notation, making sure that each main point was developed equally? Did I heed my Instructor's advice to use sources as sub or supporting points and not as main points? Did I cite all sources first and clearly? Or did I continue to use parentheses, knowing that my audience can't see these and therefore doesn't know that I'm using a source? Did I put my name and specific purpose and topic on my outline as acted? Did I attach my works cited page?
3. Did I use professional looking visual aids or did I throw something together at the last minute? Did I check my equipment beforehand so that I knew it worked or did I just assume it worked? Did I fully and clearly explain my visual so that the audience understood its significance? Did I keep my visual aid hidden until I was ready to explain it? Or did I put it up at the beginning, losing all impact because my audience was looking at it instead of listening to me?
4. Did I look at my audience, using meaningful eye contact? Or did I write a paper for another class and read that to my audience? Did I practice my speech OUT LOUD many times so that my delivery was smooth, compelling and polished? Did I use my voice and the words on the page to convince my audience that I

was committed to my topic and my information? Or did I just assume that because I was standing in front of the room that everyone would be interested in what I had to say? Did I try to involve my audience by asking questions, making my information relevant to them, and trying to give them reasons to listen throughout my speech? Or did I ignore any audience and just read what was on my cards, assuming they would see how this information might affect them?

5. Did I time my speech at home so I knew exactly how long it was, or did I not bother to do that, thinking I could "eyeball" my outline and know? Did I run way over my time, showing total disrespect for all my fellow students?

Please read this over several times and review again before you speak again

EVALUATION FORMS

Peer Review Informative Speaking

Name of student giving presentation: _____

Name of student reviewing presentation: _____

1. Student clearly opened presentation with impact.

    AGREE _____ 5 _____ 4 _____ 3 _____ 2 _____ 1 DISAGREE

2. Student clearly stated thesis statement in Introduction.

    AGREE _____ 5 _____ 4 _____ 3 _____ 2 _____ 1 DISAGREE

3. Student used visual aid effectively/Visual aid looked professional.

    AGREE _____ 5 _____ 4 _____ 3 _____ 2 _____ 1 DISAGREE

4. Student's main points were clearly stated.

    AGREE _____ 5 _____ 4 _____ 3 _____ 2 _____ 1 DISAGREE

5. Student clearly cited the correct number of sources.

    AGREE _____ 5 _____ 4 _____ 3 _____ 2 _____ 1 DISAGREE

6. Student concluded presentation by summarizing and closing with impact.

    AGREE _____ 5 _____ 4 _____ 3 _____ 2 _____ 1 DISAGREE

Please give student an overall number grade based on their presentation. _____

Please add one or two sentences offering the student CONSTRUCTIVE Criticism. Then add one or two sentences highlighting what the student's strengths were in this presentation.

Peer Review   **Informative Speaking**
___

Name of student giving presentation: _____ _____

Name of student reviewing presentation: _____

1. Student clearly opened presentation with impact.

    AGREE _____ 5 _____ 4 _____ 3 _____ 2 _____ 1 DISAGREE

2. Student clearly stated thesis statement in Introduction.

    AGREE _____ 5 _____ 4 _____ 3 _____ 2 _____ 1 DISAGREE

3. Student used visual aid effectively/Visual aid looked professional.

    AGREE _____ 5 _____ 4 _____ 3 _____ 2 _____ 1 DISAGREE

4. Student's main points were clearly stated.

    AGREE _____ 5 _____ 4 _____ 3 _____ 2 _____ 1 DISAGREE

5. Student clearly cited the correct number of sources.

    AGREE _____ 5 _____ 4 _____ 3 _____ 2 _____ 1 DISAGREE

6. Student concluded presentation by summarizing and closing with impact.

    AGREE _____ 5 _____ 4 _____ 3 _____ 2 _____ 1 DISAGREE

Please give student an overall number grade based on their presentation. _____

Please add one or two sentences offering the student CONSTRUCTIVE Criticism. Then add one or two sentences highlighting what the student's strengths were in this presentation.

Peer Review   **Informative Speaking**

Name of student giving presentation: _____

Name of student reviewing presentation: _____

1. Student clearly opened presentation with impact.

    AGREE _____ 5 _____ 4 _____ 3 _____ 2 _____ 1 DISAGREE

2. Student clearly stated thesis statement in Introduction.

    AGREE _____ 5 _____ 4 _____ 3 _____ 2 _____ 1 DISAGREE

3. Student used visual aid effectively/Visual aid looked professional.

    AGREE _____ 5 _____ 4 _____ 3 _____ 2 _____ 1 DISAGREE

4. Student's main points were clearly stated.

    AGREE _____ 5 _____ 4 _____ 3 _____ 2 _____ 1 DISAGREE

5. Student clearly cited the correct number of sources.

    AGREE _____ 5 _____ 4 _____ 3 _____ 2 _____ 1 DISAGREE

6. Student concluded presentation by summarizing and closing with impact.

    AGREE _____ 5 _____ 4 _____ 3 _____ 2 _____ 1 DISAGREE

Please give student an overall number grade based on their presentation. _____

Please add one or two sentences offering the student CONSTRUCTIVE Criticism. Then add one or two sentences highlighting what the student's strengths were in this presentation.

Peer Review   Informative Speaking

Name of student giving presentation: _____

Name of student reviewing presentation: _____

1. Student clearly opened presentation with impact.

    AGREE _____ 5 _____ 4 _____ 3 _____ 2 _____ 1 DISAGREE

2. Student clearly stated thesis statement in Introduction.

    AGREE _____ 5 _____ 4 _____ 3 _____ 2 _____ 1 DISAGREE

3. Student used visual aid effectively/Visual aid looked professional.

    AGREE _____ 5 _____ 4 _____ 3 _____ 2 _____ 1 DISAGREE

4. Student's main points were clearly stated.

    AGREE _____ 5 _____ 4 _____ 3 _____ 2 _____ 1 DISAGREE

5. Student clearly cited the correct number of sources.

    AGREE _____ 5 _____ 4 _____ 3 _____ 2 _____ 1 DISAGREE

6. Student concluded presentation by summarizing and closing with impact.

    AGREE _____ 5 _____ 4 _____ 3 _____ 2 _____ 1 DISAGREE

Please give student an overall number grade based on their presentation. _____

Please add one or two sentences offering the student CONSTRUCTIVE Criticism. Then add one or two sentences highlighting what the student's strengths were in this presentation.

| Peer Review | Persuasive/Persuasive Sales |

Name of student giving presentation: _____

Name of student reviewing presentation: _____

1. Student clearly stated thesis near the beginning of the presentation.

    AGREE _____ 5 _____ 4 _____ 3 _____ 2 _____ 1 DISAGREE

2. Student provided supporting evidence for his/her persuasive argument during presentation.

    AGREE _____ 5 _____ 4 _____ 3 _____ 2 _____ 1 DISAGREE

3. Student used clear signposts/transitions.

    AGREE _____ 5 _____ 4 _____ 3 _____ 2 _____ 1 DISAGREE

4. How effective was student's use of visual aid?

    AGREE _____ 5 _____ 4 _____ 3 _____ 2 _____ 1 DISAGREE

5. Student concluded by summarizing and closing with impact.

    AGREE _____ 5 _____ 4 _____ 3 _____ 2 _____ 1 DISAGREE

6. Student established good eye contact.

    AGREE _____ 5 _____ 4 _____ 3 _____ 2 _____ 1 DISAGREE

7. Please give student an OVERALL number grade based on overall performance (preparation, eye contact, delivery, structure, etc.).

    HIGHEST _____ 5 _____ 4 _____ 3 _____ 2 _____ 1 LOWEST

Comments: Please write at least one or two sentences offering CONSTRUCTIVE criticism. Focus on things that speaker has control over, such as use of signposts and eye contact. Relate strong points of presentation and what student might want to work on when preparing for next presentation.

Peer Review   **Persuasive/Persuasive Sales**

Name of student giving presentation: _____

Name of student reviewing presentation: _____

1. Student clearly stated thesis near the beginning of the presentation.

    AGREE _____ 5 _____ 4 _____ 3 _____ 2 _____ 1 DISAGREE

2. Student provided supporting evidence for his/her persuasive argument during presentation.

    AGREE _____ 5 _____ 4 _____ 3 _____ 2 _____ 1 DISAGREE

3. Student used clear signposts/transitions.

    AGREE _____ 5 _____ 4 _____ 3 _____ 2 _____ 1 DISAGREE

4. How effective was student's use of visual aid?

    AGREE _____ 5 _____ 4 _____ 3 _____ 2 _____ 1 DISAGREE

5. Student concluded by summarizing and closing with impact.

    AGREE _____ 5 _____ 4 _____ 3 _____ 2 _____ 1 DISAGREE

6. Student established good eye contact.

    AGREE _____ 5 _____ 4 _____ 3 _____ 2 _____ 1 DISAGREE

7. Please give student an OVERALL number grade based on overall performance (preparation, eye contact, delivery, structure, etc.).

    HIGHEST _____ 5 _____ 4 _____ 3 _____ 2 _____ 1 LOWEST

Comments: Please write at least one or two sentences offering CONSTRUCTIVE criticism. Focus on things that speaker has control over, such as use of signposts and eye contact. Relate strong points of presentation and what student might want to work on when preparing for next presentation.

Peer Review   **Persuasive/Persuasive Sales**

Name of student giving presentation: _____

Name of student reviewing presentation: _____

1. Student clearly stated thesis near the beginning of the presentation.

   AGREE _____ 5 _____ 4 _____ 3 _____ 2 _____ 1 DISAGREE

2. Student provided supporting evidence for his/her persuasive argument during presentation.

   AGREE _____ 5 _____ 4 _____ 3 _____ 2 _____ 1 DISAGREE

3. Student used clear signposts/transitions.

   AGREE _____ 5 _____ 4 _____ 3 _____ 2 _____ 1 DISAGREE

4. How effective was student's use of visual aid?

   AGREE _____ 5 _____ 4 _____ 3 _____ 2 _____ 1 DISAGREE

5. Student concluded by summarizing and closing with impact.

   AGREE _____ 5 _____ 4 _____ 3 _____ 2 _____ 1 DISAGREE

6. Student established good eye contact.

   AGREE _____ 5 _____ 4 _____ 3 _____ 2 _____ 1 DISAGREE

7. Please give student an OVERALL number grade based on overall performance (preparation, eye contact, delivery, structure, etc.).

   HIGHEST _____ 5 _____ 4 _____ 3 _____ 2 _____ 1 LOWEST

Comments: Please write at least one or two sentences offering CONSTRUCTIVE criticism. Focus on things that speaker has control over, such as use of signposts and eye contact. Relate strong points of presentation and what student might want to work on when preparing for next presentation.

Peer Review Persuasive/Persuasive Sales
___

Name of student giving presentation: _____

Name of student reviewing presentation: _____

1. Student clearly stated thesis near the beginning of the presentation.

    AGREE _____ 5 _____ 4 _____ 3 _____ 2 _____ 1 DISAGREE

2. Student provided supporting evidence for his/her persuasive argument during presentation.

    AGREE _____ 5 _____ 4 _____ 3 _____ 2 _____ 1 DISAGREE

3. Student used clear signposts/transitions.

    AGREE _____ 5 _____ 4 _____ 3 _____ 2 _____ 1 DISAGREE

4. How effective was student's use of visual aid?

    AGREE _____ 5 _____ 4 _____ 3 _____ 2 _____ 1 DISAGREE

5. Student concluded by summarizing and closing with impact.

    AGREE _____ 5 _____ 4 _____ 3 _____ 2 _____ 1 DISAGREE

6. Student established good eye contact.

    AGREE _____ 5 _____ 4 _____ 3 _____ 2 _____ 1 DISAGREE

7. Please give student an OVERALL number grade based on overall performance (preparation, eye contact, delivery, structure, etc.).

    HIGHEST _____ 5 _____ 4 _____ 3 _____ 2 _____ 1 LOWEST

Comments: Please write at least one or two sentences offering CONSTRUCTIVE criticism. Focus on things that speaker has control over, such as use of signposts and eye contact. Relate strong points of presentation and what student might want to work on when preparing for next presentation.

MONROE'S MOTIVATED SEQUENCE EVALUATION FORM

Speaker: _____ Time: _____

Topic: _____

Rate the speaker on each point:

5	4	3	2	1
excellent	good	average	fair	poor

Attention Step   Comments

_____ gained attention of listeners
_____ introduced topic clearly
_____ showed importance of topic to this audience

Need Step

_____ problem clearly explained
_____ problem demonstrated with evidence
_____ cited sufficient support, varied and relevant to the audience
_____ problem related to audience

Satisfaction Step

_____ plan clearly explained
_____ plan well thought out, demonstrated and objections met
_____ practicality proven, workability

Visualization Step

_____ benefits of plan related to audience
_____ vivid imagery used to show effects of plan

Action Step

_____ call for specific action by audience
_____ vivid concluding appeal

Delivery

_____ transitions effective
_____ extemporaneous, conversational, clear and concise language
_____ poised, confident and enthusiastic presentation
_____ nonverbal communication effective, maintained eye contact
_____ effective use of visual aid(s)

Purpose

_____ speaker's overall purpose achieved

_____TOTAL POINTS

Speech Delivery

Delivery refers to what you do with the words written on your page or your note cards. As a speaker, you can't just READ the words of your speech. Your objective is to bring the words to life. Look at your audience. Talk to your audience. Use vocal variety and intensity. Use inflection, and don't be afraid to pause. Emphasize certain words for impact. Vary your rate and pitch. Remember. Your goal is to communicate with your audience.

ARTICULATION EXERCISE

The origin of the following passage is unknown. A previous instructor has suggested that you read the passage each day until you memorize it. Recite the passage and concentrate on articulation and diction.

Generally speaking, the articulation of the population is terribly indistinct, inasmuch as it is irremediably lacking in clarity and totally indistinguishable. Nevertheless, a veritable metamorphosis indubitably took place during the months of January and February, when several practitioners in the indescribably delicate art of elocution dedicated themselves to the rehabilitation of that characteristically, particularly inarticulate percentage of our inhabitants, whose inadequacies of self-expression form so wholly redundant and superfluous a stain upon our otherwise ineffably immaculate national escutcheon.

TONGUE TWISTERS

1. Angels hang ancient anchors at angles that anger ogres.
2. Never ever offer awful Arthur alfalfa.
3. A big bug hit a bald bear and the bold bald bear bled blood badly.
4. Bruce brought big biscuits. Bob brought both briskets.
5. Bess's pet pestered Fess. (three times)
6. Bluebeard's blue bluebird. (three times)
7. Bob's blue blobs.
8. A big blue bucket of blue blackberries.
9. Bess is the best backward blue-blowing bugler in the Boston brass band.
10. A cheeky chimp chucked cheap chocolate chips in the cheap chocolate chip shop.
11. The chap in the cap clapped when he captured the cat in the trap.
12. Glenda glued Gilda's galoshes.
13. Ike ships ice chips in ice chips ships.
14. This disk sticks. (three times)
15. Much mashed mushrooms. (three times)
16. Phyllis Bickle spilled Bill Spector's sack of speckled pickles.
17. Is a pleasant peasant's pheasant present?
18. She sells seashells by the seashore.

19. Strange strategic statistics.
20. The sea ceaseth seething.
21. The sun shines on the shop signs.
22. Mr. Spink thinks the sphinx stinks.
23. If two witches watched two watches, which witch would watch which watch?
24. Come kick six sticks quick.

MORE TONGUE TWISTERS

1. "What ails Alex?" asks Alice.
2. Never ever offer awful Arthur alfalfa.
3. Alice asks for axes. Alice asks for axes. Alice asks for axes.
4. Blake the baker bakes black bread.
5. "The bun is better buttered," Buffy muttered.
6. Bess's pet pestered Fess. Bess's pet pestered Fess. Bess's pet pestered Fess.
7. I'll bet Beth's beau Brett brought Beth both bikes.
8. The best breath test tests breath better.
9. I have a black-backed bath brush. Do you have a black-backed bath brush?
10. Clean clams crammed in clean cans.
11. Top chopstick shops stock top chopsticks.
12. Tricky crickets. Tricky crickets. Tricky crickets.
13. If Sue chews shoes, should she choose to chew new shoes or old shoes?
14. Cinnamon, aluminum, linoleum. Cinnamon, aluminum, linoleum. Cinnamon, aluminum, linoleum.
15. Charles chose the chief cheap sheep section.
16. A cricket critic tricked his neck at a critical cricket match.
17. Has Hal's heel healed? Has Hal's heel healed? Has Hal's heel healed?
18. "Hello, Harry Healy," hollered Holly Hartley.
19. Ike ships ice chips in ice chips ships.
20. Literally literary. Literally literary. Literally literary.
21. Luminous aluminum. Luminous aluminum. Luminous aluminum.
22. Nine nimble noblemen nibbled nuts.
23. Peter Potter splattered a plate of peas on Patty Platt's pink plaid pants.
24. Preshrunk shirts. Preshrunk shirts. Preshrunk shirts.
25. Rough rural roads. Rough rural roads. Rough rural roads.
26. Sheila seldom sells shelled shrimps.
27. Selfish sharks sell shut shellfish.
28. She sells seashells by the seashore.

COMMON PRONUNCIATION MISTAKES

	Incorrect	Correct
arctic	ar-tick	ark-tick
candidate	can-uh-date	can-di-date
chimney	chimb-lee	chim-knee
column	col-yum	col-um
corps	corpse	core
cuisine	cue-zeen	kwi-zeen
faux-pas	fox-pass	foe-pah
gist	ghist	jist
Italian	eye-tal-yun	I [short vowel]-tal-yun
liaison	lay-uh-zon	lee-aye-zon
masochistic	mass-un-chiss-tick	mass-uh-kiss-tick
monstrous	monster-us	mon-strus
once	wunst	wuns
pique	pike	peek
police	poe-lees	puh-lees
perscription	purr-scrip-shun	pree-scrip-shun
probably	prob-lee	prob-uh-blee
regular	reg-uh-lur	reg-yuh-lur
robbery	rob-ree	rob-uh-ree
soften	soft-en	sof-en
subtle	sub-tul	sut-ul
thyme	thime	time

Hamilton Gregory, Common Pronunciation Mistakes, © 2002, McGraw-Hill. Reproduced with permission of The McGraw-Hill Companies.

Self-Critique

SAMPLE SELF–CRITIQUE #1

Critique: Informative Presentation of the Benefits of Chiropractic Care

In reflection of my speech performed on the benefits of chiropractic care I think I did disastrously. In regards to my outline, I should have organized my thoughts and ideas in a better format for easier transition between principles. I should have planned my outline more carefully. The cohesion of my presentation could also have been improved by clearly stating what I am going to talk about before I speak on the topics. I got confused about the fact that you "should" tell someone what you are going to say before saying it. I didn't want to be repetitious. However, I have learned from this experience that it is vitally important for a speaker to organize their subject material and to clearly let the audience know, beforehand, what they are going to incorporate into their speech. This helps the audience to follow you and improved transition from one step to another.

After watching my speech, I realize that I forgot to incorporate sources and state where I got my information from. This was difficult for me, as I already knew the information that I was stating; however, I should have found other information and stated my sources as clearly indicated on the speech evaluation sheet (that was given to us prior to the presentation due date), it was no secret. I simply forgot.

I also realized that I did not effectively use my visual aid. I understand that the purpose of the visual aid is to improve clarity on a subject and I went ahead and put it out before I spoke about it. I got really nervous and actually forgot to use it to explain how the nerves are encased in the vertebral column and remembered right at the end of my explanation of subluxation. Once I realized that I forgot it, I got only worse from there.

As far as my stance goes, I began to fidget about 30 seconds through the presentation. Realizing what I was doing, I became even more nervous and made an attempt to stop. I would pick my feet up and then begin to lean to my left. What was I doing?

I feel I did a few things well during my presentation. I established my credibility within the first 20 seconds and let the audience know what I was going to be talking about. I feel that I chose a topic that related to many people and by the show of hands, which let me know that those problems affect many of my peers.

The enunciation of my voice has always proven to be problematic for me. Another aspect of speech that I feel I have improved greatly upon. I used to be so quiet and reserved. Now, I feel that I have summed a little confidence and can exude my vocal enunciation. I was really excited that I spoke loudly enough for everyone to hear me!!

I really enjoy the idea of giving a presentation, but once I get up there it is a dreaded, awful experience. I obviously need a lot of improvement.

In light of the critique that is due on a peer, I choose Student X's presentation on the effects of Parkinson's disease. Student X was able to connect with the audience by using a picture of her Grandmother, who is suffering from the illness. Her introduction, "Do you remember that one person in your life," really captured the audience and led to relational motivation to listen to what she was saying. Student X also made every attempt to exhibit good eye contact with the entire audience. She used inflection in her voice and exuded excitement about her material, as well as providing useful contact information regarding Parkinson's disease Research and Organizations. Her transitions were clear and she was very professional. The one thing that I wish Student X would improve is her confidence. When she gets off track, her facial expressions show her despair. However, when she does make a mistake her facial expressions make the audience have sympathy for her. I understand that this is not something that you want to happen; it destroys the credibility of the speaker. Overall, I think that Student X did a wonderful presentation, well organized, informative and interesting.

SAMPLE SELF–CRITIQUE #2

Ever since I have been at East Carolina University I have yet to do a speech in any of my classes that I have taken. Yes, I have had to teach lessons at elementary schools and had to give presentations with a group on unit plans and things of that sort, but in no way does it compare to having to get up in front of your peers for five plus minutes and talk about a specific topic with absolutely no interaction what so ever from the audience.

Communication 2420, also known as Business and Professional Communication has given me the opportunity to step out of my little box I was in and try something that I have never done, or thought I could ever do. To be completely honest, I was going to drop the class because I was so terrified of taking it, but I decided not to take the easy way out. This was my chance to prove to myself that I could do something that I have always thought that there was no way in the world that I could do, like get up in front of a class of thirty plus people and just talk. That is just what I did, I proved myself wrong.

Looking back at the tape of my speech, it was very interesting. I noticed things that I had no clue that I was doing while I was speaking. There were positive aspects and negative aspects of my speech, just like with anything else you do. Plus no one truly enjoys seeing him or herself on videotape, or at least I know I do not.

So first things first; let's talk about the negative side of the speech and save the best parts for last. While watching the tape of myself there were many things that went on that I was completely oblivious to. For example, at the very beginning of the speech my hands were shaking so bad that I could here my fingers tapping against the podium when I was holding my note cards. Many may not be able to hear it, but I could. It might have been that I just knew to look for it. This is something that I feel I need to work on because if others were to notice it and be able to hear it then it just might distract the audience and take away from the quality of my speech. Unfortunately this is caused by a bad case of the butterflies, and I do not ever see myself being 100 percent comfortable when delivering a speech. Then there was the playing with the hair. I guess it was just something to do or it was just a habit, because I play with my hair constantly. I think the only way to prevent this from happening in the future is by pulling my hair out of my face so that I will not be able to play with it. I feel that fidgeting is just one sure sign that someone is nervous, and I did not do anything to lead people into thinking otherwise. I could not see this on tape because it was from the podium up, but I remember playing with my feet while I was standing in the front of the room, yet, another nervous action.

Now let's talk about the positive aspects of my speech. It came as a shock to me, but I feel as if I did not do too terrible. As for the verbal part of my speech, I feel it went well. As far as the actual sound of my voice, I think that it was overall good. My voice projection was very good and I feel I was very articulate. When I was listening to it on the tape I could understand everything I was saying without having to strain to hear it. At the beginning of my speech my voice was very shaky, but once again nothing but nerves can be accounted for the voice shakiness. When I was preparing for my speech I would practice on eye contact by presenting to a mirror. I think that this was a good idea because it enabled me to get a feel on how it would be when I was actually presenting. When I viewed the tape I noticed that I made good eye contact, however I felt somewhat like a bobble heads doll because I was constantly working the room with my eyes. I feel that I could have been a little bit more controlled with the eye contact and I know to be more aware of it during my next speech. Considering that during a speech you are supposed to have as much eye contact as possible I feel that I did fairly well.

It seems to me there was far more negatives than positives, but it is natural for a person to notice flaws they have way more than the positive aspects of themselves. I enjoyed this project because we were able to see and hear the other students speak and it helped me feel not so alone in the process. I also realized that I was not the only one nervous about presenting.

Looking back at all the other speakers in the class, there is one particular student who stands out, and that is Student X. I really enjoyed her speech topic because it informed all of us about a way that we can help out by adopting a greyhound dog. It hit close to home because I have adopted pets in the past and I have seen first hand what happens to the animals that do not get adopted soon enough, and it is heart breaking. As for her speech delivery, she did very well. There was some fidgeting such as, playing with her visual aid books. She held onto the books and held them in front of her and twirled them around while she was speaking. However, I think primarily this was due to nerves. At the beginning of her speech she seemed a bit frazzled because her power point would not work. I think if she had double-checked once or twice before her presentation she would have known that it was not on the disk. But on the other hand she was smart to have brought her books with her for back up visual aids. I think that she made very good eye contact throughout her entire speech. I feel that she pulled the audience in and knew her topic very well. Overall, her speech was very good. It flowed well and her transitions were noticeable. She never lost me in her speech. I always knew where she was going with it.

Overall, I feel that my speech went very well. Of course it was not perfect because there is always room for improvement, however, I think it was good considering it was my first speech that I had ever done on my own. I am really thankful that we had the tapes to look back on because it will enable me to see what I need to work on and improve in for my next speech.

EXAMPLE OF A SELF-CRITIQUE ASSIGNMENT

You must write a 2–3 page paper critiquing yourself on your speech that you watched on videotape. You must watch your speech and then write a paper reviewing the following aspects of your speech.

Organization

- Thesis
- Transitions
- Open with impact
- Close with impact
- Restate thesis
- Follow clear organizational pattern

Delivery
NONVERBAL

- Eye contact
- Use of floor
- Gestures
- Distracting mannerisms
- Posture
- Confidence
- Use of notecards

VERBAL

- Enthusiasm
- Volume
- Articulation
- Vocal Quality
- Rate
- Verbal Fillers

Credibility

Citing of Sources

Visual Aid

Overall Strengths

Overall Weaknesses